SAMSUNG GALAXY A
FOR BEGINNERS

A COMPLETE GUIDE WITH THE LATEST ANDROID TIPS & TRICKS ON HOW USE THE NEW SAMSUNG GALAXY A55 SMARTPHONE LIKE A PRO.

DAVIS MOORE

TABLE OF CONTENTS

CHAPTER ONE 19

SET UP YOUR DEVICE 19

    Maintaining water and dust resistance 19

CHARGE THE BATTERY 21

TURN ON YOUR MOBILE DEVICE 21

USING THE SETUP WIZARD 22

BRING DATA FROM AN OLD DEVICE 22

LOCK OR UNLOCK YOUR DEVICE 24

    Double press 24

    Press and hold 25

ACCOUNTS 26

    Add a Google Account 26

    Add a Samsung account 27

    Add an Outlook account 27

    Set up voicemail 27

NAVIGATION 29

NAVIGATION BAR 33

    Navigation buttons 33

    Navigation gestures 34

CUSTOMIZE YOUR HOME SCREEN 36

    App icons 36

- Wallpaper ... 36
- Themes ... 38
- Icons ... 38
- Widgets ... 39
- Customize Widgets ... 39
- Home screen settings ... 40

EASY MODE ... 43
- Status bar ... 44

NOTIFICATION PANEL ... 45
- View the Notification panel ... 45
- Quick settings ... 46
- Quick Settings icon ... 47
- Quick settings options ... 47

BIXBY ... 49
- Bixby Routines ... 49
- Bixby Vision ... 50
- Camera ... 50
- Gallery ... 50
- Internet ... 50

DIGITAL WELLBEING AND PARENTAL CONTROLS ... 51

ALWAYS ON DISPLAY ... 54

AOD themes 55

CHAPTER TWO 57
BIOMETRIC SECURITY 57

Face recognition 57

Face recognition management 58

Fingerprint scanner 59

Fingerprint management 60

Fingerprint verification settings 60

Biometrics settings 61

MOBILE CONTINUITY 63

Link to Windows 63

Link your device to your computer 64

Continue apps on other devices 65

MULTI WINDOW 66

Window controls 67

EDGE PANELS 68

Apps panel 68

Configure Edge panels 70

Edge panel position and style 71

More info about Edge panels 72

ENTER TEXT 73

Toolbar 73

Configure the Samsung keyboard 75
USE SAMSUNG VOICE INPUT 78
Configure Samsung voice input 78
EMERGENCY MODE 80
Activate Emergency mode................................... 80
Emergency mode features 81
Turn off Emergency mode 82
CHAPTER THREE 83
CAMERA AND GALLERY 83
Camera... 83
Navigate the camera screen................................ 84
Configure shooting mode 85
AR Zone 87
Single take 88
Record videos 89
Camera settings.. 90
Intelligent features... 90
GALLERY 94
View pictures... 94
Edit pictures 96
Play video 97
Share pictures and videos 98

6

Delete pictures and videos 98

Group similar images 99

TAKE A SCREENSHOT 99

Palm swipe to capture a screenshot 99

Screenshot settings.. 100

SCREEN RECORDER 101

Screen recorder settings..................................... 102

CHAPTER FOUR... 103

APPLICATIONS 103

Uninstall or disable apps..................................... 103

Search for apps 103

Sort apps 104

Create and use folders.. 104

Copy a folder to a Home screen 105

Delete a folder 105

Game Booster 106

App settings 106

SAMSUNG APPLICATIONS... 108

AR Zone 108

Bixby... 108

Galaxy Store 108

Galaxy Wearable... 108

- Game Launcher 108
- Samsung Free 109
- Samsung Global Goals 109
- Samsung TV Plus 109
- SmartThings 109
- Tips 110

CALCULATOR 111

CALENDAR 112
- Add calendars 112
- Calendar alert style 113
- Create an event 114
- Delete an event 114

CLOCK 115
- Alarm 115
- Delete an alarm 117
- Alert settings 117

WORLD CLOCK 118
- Time zone converter 119
- Weather settings 119
- Stopwatch 120
- Timer 121
- Preset timer 121

  Timer options 122

  General settings 123

CHAPTER FIVE 124

CONTACTS 124

  Create a contact 124

  Edit a contact 125

  Favorites 125

  Share a contact 126

GROUPS 127

  Create a group 127

  Add or remove group contacts 128

  Send a message to a group 128

  Send an email to a group 129

  Delete a group 129

  Merge contacts 130

  Import contacts 130

  Export contacts 131

  Sync contacts 131

  Delete contacts 132

CHAPTER SIX 133

INTERNET 133

  Browser tabs 133

    Create a Bookmark..134

    Open a Bookmark 134

    Save a web page..134

    View history..135

    Share pages..135

SECRET MODE...136

    Secret mode settings..136

    Turn off secret mode..137

    Internet settings..137

MESSAGES...138

    Message search..138

    Delete conversations..139

    Send SOS messages..139

    Message settings 140

    Emergency alerts.. 141

MY FILES.. 142

    File groups 142

    My Files settings..143

CHAPTER SEVEN..145

PHONE 145

    Calls 145

    Make a call... 146

Make a call from Recent 146

Make a call from Contacts 146

Answer a call 147

Decline a call 147

Decline with a message 147

End a call 147

Actions while on a call 148

Switch to headset or speaker 148

Multitask 148

Call background 149

Call pop-up settings 149

Manage calls 150

Call log 150

Save a contact from a recent call 151

Delete call records 151

Block a number 151

Emergency calls 152

Phone settings 153

Place a multi-party call 153

Video calls 154

SAMSUNG HEALTH 155

Before you start exercising 155

SAMSUNG NOTES ... 157
Create notes ... 158
Voice recordings ... 158
Edit notes ... 158
Notes options ... 159
SAMSUNG PAY ... 160
Use Samsung Pay ... 160
Quick access ... 161
Use gift cards with Samsung Pay ... 162
GOOGLE APPS ... 163
Chrome ... 163
Drive ... 163
Duo ... 163
Gmail ... 163
Google ... 163
Messages ... 164
Photos ... 164
Play Store ... 164
SETTINGS ... 165
Access Settings ... 165
Search for Settings ... 165
Wi-Fi Connections ... 166

Connect to a hidden Wi-Fi network 166

   Wi-Fi Direct 168

   Disconnect from Wi-Fi Direct 168

NFC AND PAYMENT 169

DATA USAGE 170

   Turn on Data saver 170

   Monitor mobile data 171

   Monitor Wi-Fi data 172

MOBILE HOTSPOT 173

   Configure mobile hotspot settings 174

   Auto hotspot 175

TETHERING 175

   Connect to a printer 176

VIRTUAL PRIVATE NETWORKS 177

   Manage a VPN 177

   Connect to a VPN 178

SOUNDS AND VIBRATION 179

   Sound mode 179

   Vibrations 180

   Volume 180

   Use Volume keys for media 181

   Media volume limit 181

Ringtone 182

Notification sound 182

System sounds and vibration 183

NOTIFICATIONS 185

Notification pop-up style..................................... 185

DO NOT DISTURB.. 186

Alert when phone picked up 187

DISPLAY.. 188

Dark mode... 188

Screen brightness 189

Motion smoothness 189

Eye comfort shield 190

Screen mode 191

Font size and style... 191

Screen zoom 192

Full screen apps... 192

Screen timeout 192

Accidental touch protection...............................193

Touch sensitivity 193

Show charging information 193

Screen saver.. 194

Lift to wake.. 195

Double tap to turn on & off screen 195

Keep screen on while viewing 195

One-handed mode 196

LOCK SCREEN AND SECURITY 197

Screen lock types 197

Set a secure screen lock 197

Clock and information 199

Google Play Protect 200

FIND MY MOBILE 201

Turn on Find My Mobile 201

Find My Device 202

Permission manager 202

SAMSUNG PASS 204

Secure Folder 204

Install unknown apps 205

Encrypt or decrypt SD card 205

Decrypt SD card 206

Set up SIM card lock 206

View passwords 207

Introduction

As a beginner or senior user, this book will enhance your smartphone knowledge and also help you get the most out of your device.

This book is a comprehensive step by step guide with photographs that will enable you to easily operating or find settings on the smartphone and it also contains numerous advanced features of the Galaxy A55 that are rarely seen elsewhere.

It's satisfactory for all level of beginner and senior.

Copyright 2024 © Davis Moore

All rights reserved. This book is copyrighted and no part of it may be reproduced, stored, or transmitted, in any form or means, without the prior written permission of the copyright owner. Printed in the United States of America.

Copyright 2024 © Davis Moore

Galaxy A55 Layout

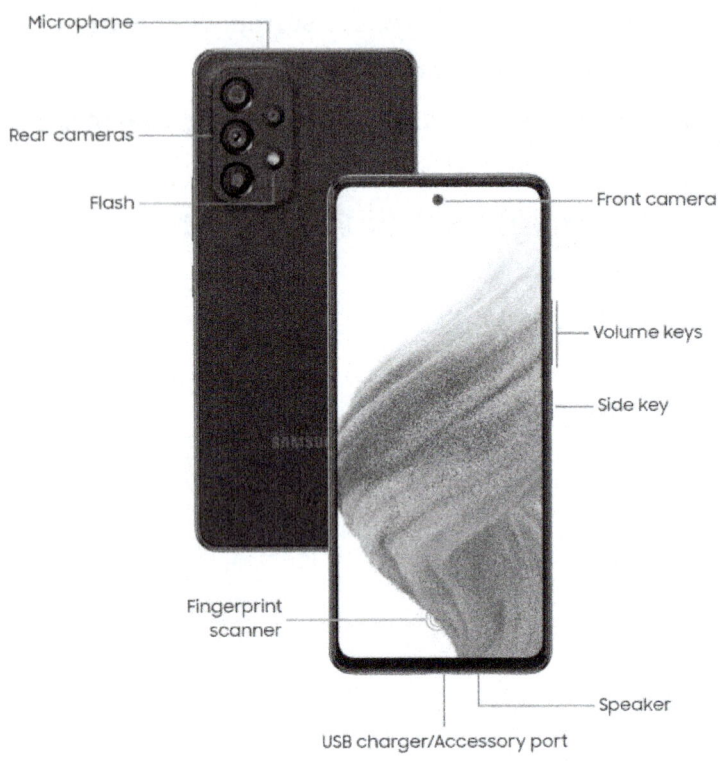

CHAPTER ONE
SET UP YOUR DEVICE

The default SIM card for your mobile device is a Nano SIM card. If a SIM is not preinstalled on your smartphone, you can use your previous SIM card.

Maintaining water and dust resistance

WARNING: If your gadget is wet or come in contact with water, do not charge it. Doing so may result to electric shock.

To maintain water and dust resistant or to keep your gadget from severe damage read the instructions below carefully:

- To prevent water or any liquid from getting into the SIM card tray of the smartphone, close the SIM card tray very tight.
- If the speaker of your device is wet or the device fell inside water, sounds may not be heard clearly during calls. If this happens clean the device with a dry soft towel before using it.
- If the smartphone is hot, do not deep it inside water.

- The water and dust resistant feature of this gadget may be damaged if the gadget gets broken.

NOTE: If liquid like oil or other liquid apart from fresh water gets into your gadget, do well to wash it with fresh water and dry it thoroughly to avoid damage to the gadget.

CHARGE THE BATTERY

Before turning on the gadget, make sure the battery is completely charged.

NOTE: Only Samsung approved charger, batteries and accessories should be used on your gadget to prevent damages.

TIP: When charging your mobile device and the charger eventually becomes hot, don't panic, this does not affect the gadget lifespan, all you need do is to detach the charger from the gadget and allow it to cool down.

TURN ON YOUR MOBILE DEVICE

To turn your gadget on, Use the Side key (button) located at the side of your gadget.

- To turn on the gadget while shutdown, press and hold the side key for some seconds.

- ⏻ Power off button will appear on your screen when your press the Side key and the Volume downward key at the same time to shut down the gadget.

- ⟳ Restart button will display on the gadget screen, when you press the Side key and the Volume down key.

USING THE SETUP WIZARD

When you turn on the gadget for the first time, the Setup Wizard feature will guide you on how to set up the mobile device.

Follow the Setup Wizard instruction to choose a default language, join a Wi-Fi network and choose locations service and more.

BRING DATA FROM AN OLD DEVICE

Data like (Images, Videos, Music, Documents and other files) from your old gadget can be transferred to your new gadget using the Smart Switch feature. You can also transfer data between both device by using via a USB cable, Computer or Wi-Fi. For more info on how this feature works, visit Samsung.com/smartswitch.

1. Unlock the gadget if you enable a lock screen on it and go to the Setting app, tap ⟳

Accounts and backup > Bring data from old device.

2. Select a file to transfer and follow the prompts.

LOCK OR UNLOCK YOUR DEVICE

Other people will not be able to access your gadget if you set up a secure lock screen. The mobile device will lock automatically when the screen times out.

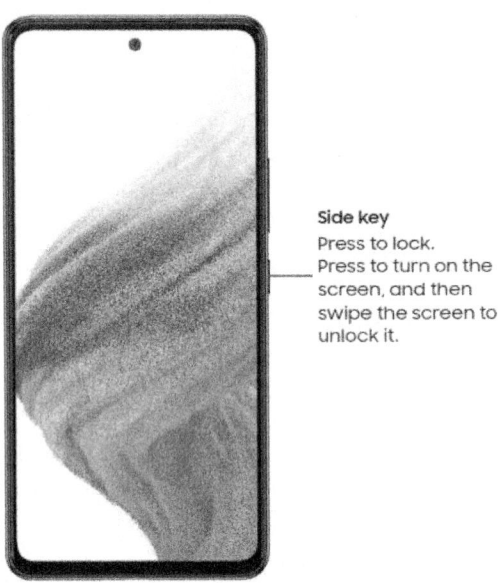

Side key
Press to lock.
Press to turn on the screen, and then swipe the screen to unlock it.

Double press

Some features on your gadget can be activated if the Side key is pressed twice.

1. Unlock the gadget if you have set up a screen lock, and head straight to the Settings application, tap ◯ Advanced features and then click Side key.

2. Choose the "Double press" option and select a feature to be activated when you press the Side key twice:
- You can launch the Camera.
- Select an app to launch when you press the Side key twice.

Press and hold

Some apps and features can be activated when the Side key pressed for a long time.

1. Unlock the gadget if it has a screen lock enabled on it and go to the Settings app, select Advanced features and then click Side key.
2. Select the option "Double press" and choose a feature to be activate when the Side key is pressed for a long time:
- The feature "Bixby" can be activated if your press and Side key for long.
- The power off menu will appear when you also press and hold the Side key.

ACCOUNTS

Account can be added and managed on your gadget.

TIP: Accounts may support the following:

- Calendars
- Contacts
- Emails and other features.

Add a Google Account

After signing into your Google account, you will be able to install apps from the Google Play Store and also purchases items.

Set up a lock screen after signing into your Google account to turn on the Google Device Protection feature.

This same account will be needed if you want to carry out a factory data reset.

1. To set up and manage an account on your gadget, go to the Settings app, select Accounts and backup and then tap Manage accounts.

2. Under the Add account menu select Google.

Add a Samsung account

Sign in or create a new Samsung account so that you can have access to the special features of Samsung and use the apps on Samsung fully.

- o Setting up a Samsung account is very easy, all you need do is, go the Settings app and select Samsung account.

Add an Outlook account

All emails going in and out of your gadget can be managed in the Outlook account.

1. To set up or create an outlook account on your gadget, open the Settings app, select Accounts and backup and then click Manage accounts.

2. Under the ╋ Add account session, select Outlook.

Set up voicemail

Set up this service after turning on your gadget for the first time of setting up your device. From the Phone app you can access this feature.

1. Unlock the gadget if it has a screen lock enabled in it and launch the ⓒ Phone app, after launching the Phone app press and hold 1 or touch the ⌣ Voicemail icon.

2. To create a password, record a greeting or name, follow the onscreen prompts.

NAVIGATION

Touch your gadget slightly and it will respond. Don't use objects metallic to touch the screen or apply pressure on the screen, doing so may cause damage to the screen. If your screen gets damaged due on excessive force or metallic object, it will not be covered by Samsung warranty.

Tap

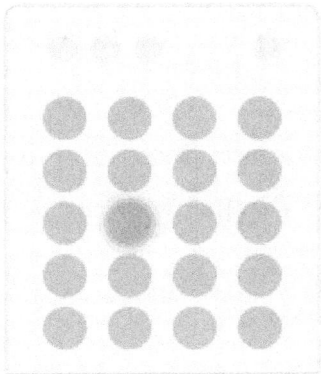

Click on items or icons to activate them.

- Touch an application icon to launch the app.
- Touch the screen twice quickly to zoom in or out on an object.

Swipe

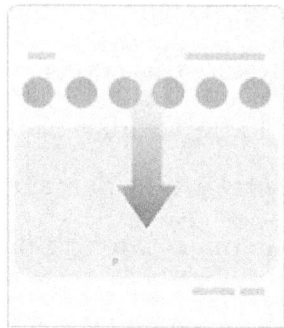

Move your fingertip across the screen calmly.

- To unlock your gadget, swipe upward from the Lock screen.
- To view through the home screen and Apps screen swipe to the left or right.

Drag and drop

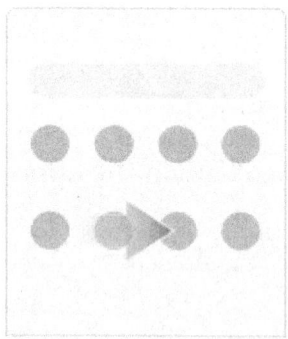

To move item to a new position on your gadget, press and hold the item and move it.

- To add an application shortcut to the Home screen of your gadget, simply drag it.
- Drag a widget to move it to a new location.

Zoom in and out

Move two of your fingers apart or together to zoom in or out on an object.

- Move your thumb and any other finger together to zoom out.
- Move your thumb and any other finger apart to zoom in.

Touch and hold

To activate items, press and hold them

- Once an item is pressed and held, it will display a pop-up menu of options.
- Once a blank space in the Home screen is pressed and held, you will be able to customize it.

NAVIGATION BAR

There are two types of navigation, which are the "Full Screen Navigation" and the "Buttons Navigation" you can use it navigation buttons to move around the device screen.

Navigation buttons

Use the buttons that are located at the bottom of your gadget to navigate around the screen.

1. To navigate around the mobile device, use the navigation buttons. Go to the Settings

app, Select the ⚙ Display options, click Navigation bar and then tap Buttons.

2. To place your Back and Recent buttons where you want them, select an option under Button order.

Navigation gestures

Navigate around the screen using the navigation gestures to avoid being obstructed when making use of your gadget.

1. To use the navigation gesture to navigate around the device screen, launch the settings application after unlocking your screen if it has a screen lock, select ⚙ Display, tap Navigation bar and then select Swipe gestures to enable the navigation feature.

2. Choose an option below to customize:

- More options: Choose the Sensitivity and pattern of a gesture.
- Gesture hint: Set your gadget to show lines at the bottom of your screen.

- Show button to hide keyboard: To hide the keyboard while your gadget is put in portrait mode, show icons on the lower right corner of the screen of the gadget.

CUSTOMIZE YOUR HOME SCREEN

You can set your Home screen in many ways, as setting up widgets and adding favorite programs to the Home page.

App icons

Touch an icon for an app to open it from the Home screen.

- To add an app icon to the Home screen, press and hold its icon and select ⊕ Add to Home on the Apps screen.

To remove an icon:

- On a Home screen, press and hold an applications icon, and then click Remove.

NOTE: Your gadget still retains apps that their icons are removed from the Home screen.

Wallpaper

Choose a default image or select an image or video from your Gallery to set it as your Home or Lock screen wallpaper.

1. When you press and hold any screen on the Home screen, the option "Wallpaper and Style" will appear click on it.
2. To view available wallpapers, select one of the menus below:
- Choose from wallpapers that are available on your gadget by default.
- Choose an image or video from your gadget's Gallery app.
- Choose a palette based on the colors of your gadget's wallpaper.
- Apply Dark theme to Wallpaper.
- Go to the Galaxy Themes menu and download more beautiful and glowing wallpapers.
3. To choose a photo or video, touch it.
- You can select to apply a single photo to the Home or Lock screen.
- You can select to apply multiple images to the Home or Lock screen.
- Select one or multiple images or videos in your Gallery app and select Done.

Themes

Choose a theme that you want to apply to your gadget's Home or Lock screen, wallpapers and app icons.

1. Hold an open space while on the Home screen.
2. To preview a theme before downloading it, select 🖌 Themes, and choose a theme.
3. Downloaded themes will appear when you select My stuff then tap Themes under ☰ Menu.
4. To use the theme, you have selected on your gadget, touch Apply.

Icons

Your gadget's default icons can be changed

1. Hold an open space while on the Home screen.
2. To preview an icon before downloading it, select 🖌 Themes and tap Icons.
3. To view all the icons that you have downloaded, select ☰ Menu and tap My stuff then Icons.

4. Touch Apply to use the select icon on your gadget.

Widgets

Information and apps will have easy access if their widgets are added to the Home screen.

1. Hold an open space while on your Home screen.
2. Select the Widget you want to apply to your Home screen under ⚏ Widget.
3. Choose Add after choosing the widget to be applied to your home screen.

Customize Widgets

To positioning and performance of an added widget can be customized.

- o Press and hold a widget from the Home screen and choose and option:

- 🗑 Delete: Press the delete symbol to remove the widget that you don't want.

- ⚙ Settings: Press the Settings symbol to make changes to the widget on your Home screen.

- ⓘ App info: Confirm the details of the widget.

Home screen settings

Beautify your Home screen and your Apps screen.

1. Unlock the gadget if it has a lock and go to the Home screen then press and hold a screen that is empty.

2. The following options can be customized when your tap ⚙ Settings:

- Layout of the Home screen: You can set your gadget to have a Home screen where all apps are displayed or have an Apps screen and a Home screen.

- Home screen grid: Pick a layout to determine how apps are sorted in the Home screen.

- Apps screen grid: Pick a layout to determine how apps are sorted in the Apps screen.

- Folder grid: Pick a layout to determine how folders are arranged.

- Add media page to Home screen: Enable this feature so that a media page will appear when you swipe to right on the Home screen. Touch to view media services that are available.

- Show Apps screen button on Home screen: For easy access to the Apps menu, set your gadget to have the apps screen button on the Home screen.
- Lock Home screen layout: This feature prevents items on your Home screen from being moved or replaced on your Home screen.
- Include new applications to Home screen: Your gadget can be allowed to display newly installed apps on the Home screen automatically.
- Secret apps: Your private apps can be hidden from the Home screen or Apps screen. Go to the Hidden apps screen to restore all apps that were hidden. While searching on the Apps screen search bar, hidden apps can appear as a result.
- App icon badges: Permit the display of badges on apps with notifications. The badge format can be customized.

- Swipe down for notification panel: Activate this feature so that you can view the notifications panel by swiping down on any screen of your gadget.
- Rotate to landscape mode: Enable this mode to automatically switch your gadget from portrait mode to landscape.
- About Home screen: Confirm your Home screen version details.

EASY MODE

This feature grants you a better visual experience while using your gadget. Icons and texts in this mode are larger.

1. Unlock the gadget if it has a lock and go to the Settings application then select ⚙ Display and tap Easy mode

2. Select ⬤ to enable this feature, then you will see the following:

- Press and hold delay: You can set hoe long for a press to be recognized on your gadget.
- Keyboard with high contrast: From here, you can choose a keyboard that has high contrast.

Status bar

Launch the Status bar to see the following.

Status icons

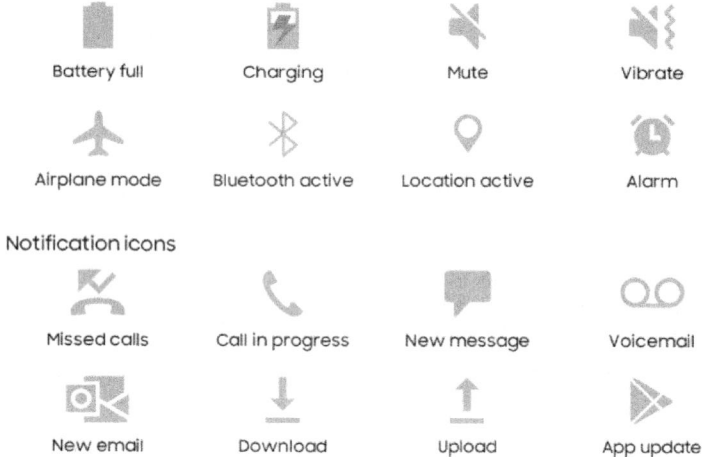

TIP: Enter the Quick settings menu and select the ⋮ More options menu then select Status bar, to be able to configure the option for your status bar to display.

NOTIFICATION PANEL

From the "Notification Panel" notifications and settings can be opened easily.

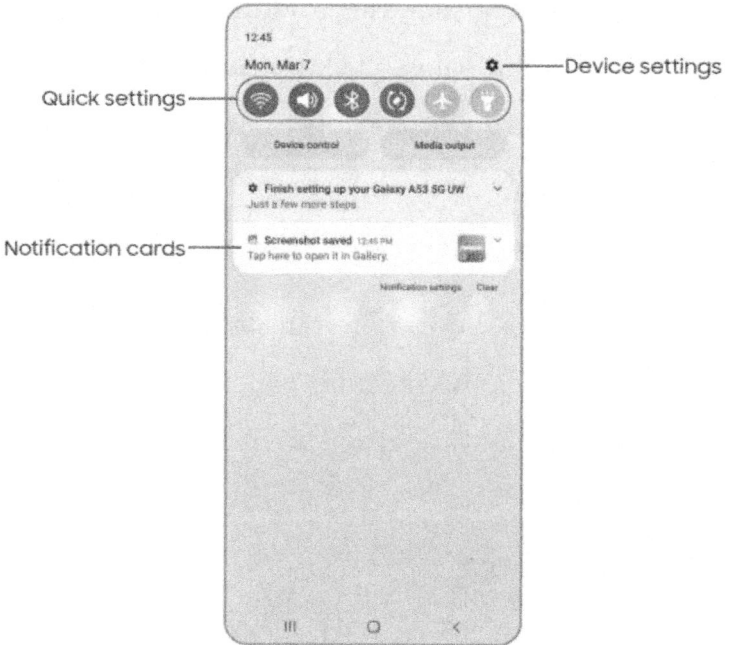

View the Notification panel

From any screen on your gadget, you can view the notification panel.

1. From the top of the screen you are in, swipe downwards to reveal the notification panel.

- Select a notification to open.

- To delete a notification from the Notification panel, drag it to the right or left side of the notification panel.
- To delete all the notifications in the notification panel, click on the clear all option at the bottom of the notification.
- To change the appearance and settings of notification, select "Notification Settings".

2. The ‹Back button of your gadget can be used to close the notification panel by tapping it or swiping upward from the bottom of your screen.

Quick settings

Settings like the Wi-Fi, Dark mode, Auto rotate, do not Disturb and power saving mode as well as other can be accessed from the Quick settings menu. the below are item that can be found in the Quick settings screen.

- o From the notification panel, swipe downward again to display the Quick settings screen.
- Touch a quick setting to turn it on or off.

- To enter a quick setting menu, press and hold it.

Quick Settings icon

Quick settings options

Go to the Quick setting to access the following.

- Finder search: Use this feature to locate apps on your gadget.

- Power off: Press the Side key for some time to power off your device.

- Open settings: Touch a setting to quickly view it.

- More options: Rearrange quick settings.

- Device control: If you have Google Home or Smart Thing installed on your gadget, you can control other devices.

- Media output: Once any audio or video device is connected, you can control the playback format.
- Brightness slider: To change the brightness of your screen, drag the slider.

BIXBY

With this feature active, you can use your gadget more effectively, the Bixby feature learns your daily habit, adapts to you, perform other tasks and set up reminder also. For more information, visit samsung.com/us/support/owners/app/Bixby.

o From the Home screen page, press and hold the Side key to launch the Bixby feature.

TIP: The Bixby feature can also be opened from the Apps list.

Bixby Routines

This Bixby feature is also capable of showing your details or changing your gadget settings based on your location.

1. Unlock the gadget and click on the Advanced features option then select Bixby Routines under the Settings app
2. To create a new routine, select "Add routine" and follow the prompts.

Bixby Vision

Your gadget automatically links the Bixby vision app with the Gallery, Camera and Internet app to give you a better experience of what is in view.

Camera

You can see the Bixby Vision in the camera viewfinder.

- Launch the 🎥 Camera app from the Home or Apps screen the select More > Bixby Vision and follow the prompts.

Gallery

From the Gallery app, you can use the Bixby vision on images and videos stored on it.

1. Select a picture or video in the ✻ Gallery app to view it.
2. Select the 👁 Bixby Vision icon and follow the prompts.

Internet

You can also use the Bixby vision feature to locate contents in the Internet app.

1. Unlock the gadget and go straight to the Internet app then press and hold an image till you see a pop-up menu.

2. Select the option "Search with Bixby Vision" then follow the onscreen prompts.

DIGITAL WELLBEING AND PARENTAL CONTROLS

Set up this feature to manage your habit digitally, by receiving a daily view of how many notifications are received and how frequent certain apps are put to use and also how frequent your gadget is checked.

- The Digital wellbeing and Parental Control menu can be accessed from the gadget's settings app.

- Click on the app dashboard to access the following options:

  - Screen time: From here, you can see the length of screen time an application was opened and made use of that day.

- Received notifications: Notifications that were received daily from a certain app can be checked from here.
- Times opened/Unlocks: Check the number of times a day an app was opened.

Your goals

- Screen time: A screen time goal can be set, of which you can also check your daily average.
- App timers: An app usage daily limit can be set.

Ways to disconnect

- Focus mode: With this mode turned on, you can limit the usage of apps for a set period of time to prevent your gadget from distraction.
- Bedtime mode: You can choose a particular time for the gray scale to be adjusted and mute calls, alert and notification and sound that may occur on your gadget.

Comfort care

- Volume check: Select a source that will manage your volume and keep your ears safe.

- Driving check: IF your gadget is connected to a car Bluetooth, you can monitor your screen and view apps that are used frequently.

Check on your kids

- Parental controls: Install the Google's Link app to monitor the technological life of your kids. From this same app you can, choose applications, create content filters, keep track of the screen time and choose a screen time limit.

ALWAYS ON DISPLAY

Your phone can stay locked while you view missed calls, messages, notification, time, date and other details, if the Always on Display feature is activated on your gadget.

1. This feature can be accessed from the gadget's Settings app when your select 🔒 Lock screen and tap Always On Display

2. To get this feature started and functioning click on the ⬤ On icon:

- When your screen is not in use, choose when to show a clock and notification on the screen of the Gadget.

- Clock style: The color option and the clock style can be changed.

- Display details of music: If the Face Widget music manager is busy, set your gadget to show the music details.

- Screen orientation: Display this mode either in Portrait or Landscape mode.

- Auto brightness: Your gadget can be set to adjust the Always on Display brightness automatically.

- About Always on Display: Check the license information and the version of software of the Always on Display.

NOTE: Some settings may appear on the Always on Display screen or the Home screen.

AOD themes

Do the following to apply custom themes for Always On Display (AOD).

1. To apply a theme to the Always on Display screen, go to the Home screen and press and hold a blank space then select 🖌 Themes and tap AODs.

- To preview a theme, you want to download to My Always on Display, select "Always on Display".

2. To view all the themes that you have downloaded, select the ≡ Menu option and hit "My stuff".

3. Touch "Apply" after selecting an ADO theme to be applied.

CHAPTER TWO
BIOMETRIC SECURITY

Logging into account and opening your gadget securely and safely can be done when you set up a biometric lock on the same gadget.

Face recognition

You face can be used to unlock your gadget securely if it has been enrolled. A PIN, Pattern or Password lock must be activated on your gadget before this feature can be put to work.

- You need to know that the face recognition process in terms of security is not in any way compared to the PIN, Pattern and Password as your gadget can be unlocked by someone of the same resemblance of you.
- There might be malfunctioning of the face recognition process, if hats, glasses, beards or heavy make-ups are worn.
- To ensure proper enrollment of the face recognition, your face should be registered in an area with sufficient light, and make sure that your camera lens is clean.

1. To set up a face recognition unlock on your gadget, unlock your gadget and go to the Settings application and select the ⭕ Biometrics and security option then click Face recognition.
2. To enroll your face on your gadget, follow the easy step on the screen accordingly.

Face recognition management

- To manage the function of the face recognition process, launch the Settings app from the Apps Screen, Home screen or the notification panel then click ⭕ Biometrics and security then tap Face recognition.
  - Remove the info of faces that have been registered before.
  - For face recognition improvement, you can add an optional appearance.
  - Turn the face unlock security on or off.
  - Open your eyes so that the face scanner can scan your face properly.

- For your face to be detected in an environment with insufficient light, all you need do is brighten your screen.
- Get more details on how the biometric lock works on your gadget.
- Get more details on hoe face recognition works on your gadget.

Fingerprint scanner

You can open your device and certain apps with your fingerprint without entering a Password, PIN or Pattern.

Your fingerprint, once enrolled can be used for verification of identity when logging into your Samsung account, but to use your fingerprint effectively on your gadget, you will need to set up a PIN, Pattern or Password on the same gadget.

1. To set up fingerprint on this gadget, go to the Settings app, select the option labeled ⭕ Biometrics and security then tap Fingerprints
2. To enroll your fingerprint, follow the easy steps on your screen.

Fingerprint management

- To manage your fingerprint recognition process on your gadget, you can just go to the Settings (Preferences) app the select Biometrics and security > Fingerprints for the options under:
  - While at the top of your fingerprint list, you will see the list of fingerprints that have been enrolled. Choose one from the list to either delete it or rename it.
  - Include new fingerprint: For another fingerprint to be enrolled, you can simply follow the easy steps on the screen.
  - Confirm added fingerprints: To ensure if a fingerprint has been added to your gadget, scan the fingerprint first.

Fingerprint verification settings

You can use your fingerprint to verify when unlocking your phone or other supported application.

- To use your fingerprint for verification while unlocking your gadget or certain app, launch the Settings app, click ⬤ Biometrics and security > Fingerprints.
  - Fingerprint unlock: Register your fingerprint to unlock your gadget with it.
  - Fingerprint active always: Put your finger on the scanner to wake your screen.
  - Display icons on the off screen: Configure the display of fingerprint icon when the screen is off.
  - Show unlocking animation: Set to show an animation if you use fingerprint to unlock your gadget.
  - Learn more about the biometric unlock.
  - Learn more about the fingerprint unlock.

Biometrics settings

- To change your settings for the biometric security, open the Settings application, click ⬤ Biometrics and security > More biometrics settings for the following option:

- Show transition effects when unlocking: Show a transition when your gadget is unlocked with the biometric process.

MOBILE CONTINUITY

The "Mobile Continuity" is also another feature on your gadget that enables you to have full access to your device storage and other features of your gadget from Smartphone and computers that are compatible.

Link to Windows

From a PC (Personal Computer) that your gadget is synced to, you can view images and messages of your gadget.

Pictures

- Drag and drop the images in windows.
- From your Photos application, you can open and edit images.
- Through windows, you can transfer photos with your contact.

Messages (SMS/MMS)

- You can set the windows to pop-up if a new message is received.

Notifications

- While on the PC (Personal Computer) that your gadget is linked to, you can view and manage notifications on your gadget.

- Decline notifications or messages that are coming from individual gadget apps.

- You can set the windows to pop-up when a new notification is received.

App mirroring

- Still on the PC that your gadget is linked to, you can live stream your gadget.

- To connect to your device, use the keyboard or the mouse.

- Use the Windows Accessibility.

Link your device to your computer

1. To sync your gadget to a PC, launch the Settings application and click on ⚙ Advanced features > Link to Windows.

2. To connect your gadget to the PC, follow the easy steps that will appear on the screen.

NOTE: This feature can also be turned on from the Quick Settings screen.

Continue apps on other devices

From other device signed into your Samsung account, you can continue apps like the Samsung Notes and the Samsung Internet app for they are supported.

1. To do this, go to the Settings screen on your Gadget and choose the option labeled Advanced features > Continue apps on other devices.
2. Select the activation icon to start this program.
3. While on your gadget, log in to your account created with Samsung.

MULTI WINDOW

The "Multi Window" feature on this your gadget can enable you to use different app on the same time, apps that supports this feature will appear on the split screen, the size of apps window can also be changed.

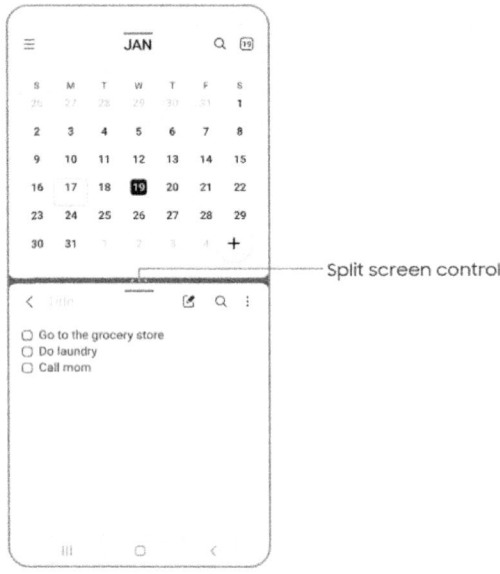
Split screen control

1. Select the ||| Recent button on the screen.
2. Click the icon of the apps then select open in Split screen view.
3. Choose an app in the other widow to put it in the split screen view also.

- Dag the center of the widow borders the change the size of the window.

Window controls

1. Drag the center of the window border to adjust the window size.
2. Tap the center of the window border for the following options:

- ↑↓ Switch window: This icon should be tapped to switch windows.

- ⊞ Add app pair: To add to Apps panel or Edge panel another app pair shortcut, click the icon.

EDGE PANELS

Your gadget features a capacity known as the Edge panel which allows you to access frequently used applications/programs, tasks, and contacts as well as viewing news, sport and others easily.

- o The Edge panel is easy to access and enable on the gadget, just go to the Settings application and select ⚙ Display then Edge panels and touch the ⬤ On icon to activate.

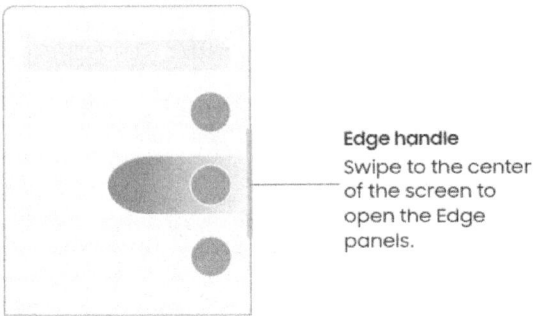

Edge handle
Swipe to the center of the screen to open the Edge panels.

Apps panel

The Apps panel, apps that you use more often can be added.

1. To access the Apps panel from any screen, drag the Edge handle to the midpoint of the screen and continue swiping.

2. To open an app and or an app pair shortcut, click on it.

3. To view the full apps list, click on ⋮⋮⋮ All app under the ≡ Menu option.

- For additional windows to be added to the pop-up view, drag the app icon from the Apps panel.

Do the following to configure Apps panel:

1. To launch the Apps panel from any screen, drag the Edge handle to the midpoint of the screen and continue swiping.

2. To add app to the Apps panel, select ≡ Menu and click ✎ Edit.

- Launch the Apps panel then press and hold an empty space then choose the app you want to add the Apps panel.
- Drag an application from the left side of the device screen on upper part of an app in the columns on the right to create a folder of apps in the Apps panel.

- To change the manner in which apps are arranged, drag apps to the location you want.

- Select the icon for ⊖ Remove to remove an app from the Apps panel.

3. To save all that you have done in the Apps panel click ⟨ Back/Navigate up button.

Configure Edge panels

1. To customize the Edge panels, go to the Display menu under Settings and select Edge panel and tap Panels.

2. The following options will appear:

- ✓ Checkbox: Each panel can be turned on or off from here.

- Edit (if available): Each panel can be edited.

- 🔍 Search: Installed panels can be searched for with this feature.

- ⋮ More options:

- Rearrange: Drag panel to the left or right.

- Uninstall: From your gadget, delete panels that are installed.
- Hide on Lock screen: If you set a secure screen, choose panels to hide on the Lock screen.
- Samsung Galaxy Store: Look for more Edge panels and download them.
3. To save all the changes that you have made select the Back/Navigate up button.

Edge panel position and style

- To change the position of the Edge handle, open Settings app and click Display then tap Edge panels > Handle for the options underneath:
- Edge handle: To change the Edge handle location, drag it along the edge of the screen.
- Position: Choose either left or right where the edge handle is to appear on.
- Lock handle position: Turn on this to avoid the Edge handle from being moved when you press and hold it.

- Style: Choose a color for the Edge handle.
- Transparency: Drag the transparency slider to change the Edge panel transparency.
- Size: To change the size of the Edge handle, drag the size slider.
- Width: To adjust the width of the Edge handle, drag the width slider.

More info about Edge panels

o To check the current software version details of the Edge panel, go to the Settings app and click Display > tap Edge panels > tap About Edge panels.

ENTER TEXT

Text can be entered on your gadget by typing or speaking.

Expand toolbar

Toolbar

Some keyboard features can be accessed from here.

- o To access all the Samsung keyboard features on your gadget, select ••• Expand toolbar:

  - ☺ Expression: Compose a message with Emoji and GIFs.

- ⌨ Clipboard: The clipboard grants you quick access to text that you have copied.

- ⌨ Modes: Choose a new layout for your keyboard.

- 🎤 Voice input: Use this feature to enter text with your voice.

- ⚙ Settings: View all the settings that are associated with the Samsung keyboard.

- 🔍 Search: From your conversations (chats) words can be searched for with the search feature.

- 🔤 Translate: Change words to your own language of understanding.

- ▶ YouTube: Get exclusive and trending videos.

- 😊 Emoji: Include emoji to your text for the purpose of fun.

- GIFs: Animated GIFs can be used from here.
- Bitmoji: Create a custom emoji and use it as your sticker.
- Mojitok: Create a custom sticker.
- AR Emoji: Create a custom emoji and make use of it in stickers.
- Keyboard size: Make the keyboard larger or smaller.

Configure the Samsung keyboard

o Launch the Samsung keyboard menu and select the Settings option for the following options to customize the keyboard:
- Languages and types: Choose a keyboard language type.
- You can easily change between languages, by swiping the tip of your finger to the left or right across the space bar on the keyboard.

Smart typing

- Predictive text: As you type words on your keyboard Suggestions will appear.
- Suggest emoji: If the predictive text feature is turned on, emoji suggestions will also appear.
- Suggest stickers while typing: While typing is ongoing, suggested stickers will appear.
- Automatic replacement: With the predictive text suggestion, you can replace text that you've typed automatically.
- Suggest text corrections: Suggest corrections of words that are spelled wrongly.
- Text shortcuts: Create a custom shortcut for words that you often use.
- More typing options: Set more options for typing.

Style and layout

- Keyboard toolbar: Allow the keyboard toolbar to be seen or hidden.
- High contrast keyboard: Change the color of the keyboard.

- Theme: Choose a theme to be used for your keyboard.
- Mode: Choose either portrait or landscape mode for your keyboard.
- Size and transparency: Change your keyboard transparency and size.
- Layout: Allow special characters to appear on your keyboard.
- Font size: Modify the size of your fonts.
- Custom symbols: The shortcuts of symbols can be changed.

Other settings

- Swipe, touch, and feedback: Feedback and gestures can be changed.
- Select third-party content to use: Third party keyboard can be allowed.
- Reset to default settings: Take the keyboard back to its original settings.
- About Samsung keyboard: See other legal info and the version of the Samsung keyboard.

USE SAMSUNG VOICE INPUT

You can enter text on your gadget without using the keyboard to type but with your voice.

- Click 🎤 Voice input and say what you want to input on the Samsung keyboard.

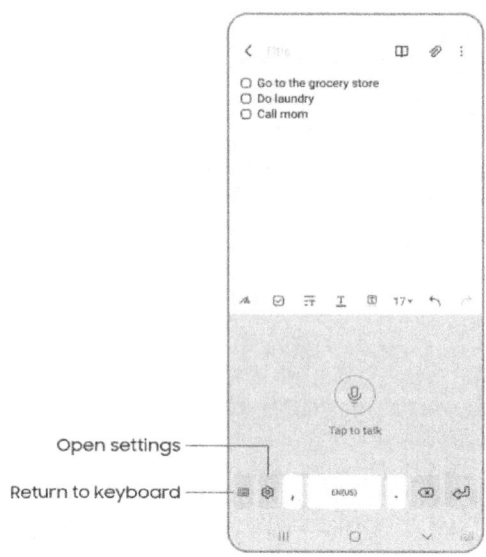

Configure Samsung voice input

1. Choose the 🎤 Voice input icon on the Samsung keyboard.

2. For more options select the icon for ⚙ Settings.

- Keyboard language: Choose a language type for the keyboard.
- Voice input language: Select a language for the Voice input.
- Hide offensive words: Block words that are offensive.
- About Samsung voice input: See the legal info and the version of the voice input.

EMERGENCY MODE

While in a case of emergency, this feature helps you to call for help even when your phone is locked.

To conserve battery power, Emergency mode:

- Limit the usage of some certain apps.
- Turn off all connectivity.

Activate Emergency mode

To turn this feature, follow the below steps:

1. Together, press and hold the Side and the Volume downward key.
2. Select the icon for 🔘 Emergency mode.
- If that is the first time that you are using it, make sure you read and accept the terms and condition.
3. Choose "Turn on".

TIP: The Emergency mode can be turned on from the Settings screen, all you need do is to go to the Settings application and select the 🔘 Safety and emergency button then select Emergency mode and turn it on using the steps that are displayed on screen.

Emergency mode features

You can only use the apps and features that are shown below when the emergency mode is activated.

- Estimated battery life: The remaining life of the battery of the gadget will appear.
- Flashlight: Make uses of the "Flashlight" while you in a dark arena.
- Emergency alarm: Make a sound.
- Phone: Go to the call screen of your gadget
- Share/Message my location: To emergency contacts, share your current location details.
- Internet/Chrome: Go to the Internet.
- Emergency call: Without a network service you can call for emergency.
- ⋮More preferences:
- Turn off Emergency mode: To take your device back to its normal mode of operation, turn off the "Emergency Mode".
- Edit apps: Add app to the screen for easy access to them and maybe remove them.

- Emergency contacts: Manage your medical profile and ICE group contacts.
- Settings: Configure the settings that are available.

Turn off Emergency mode

Your gadget will switch to its normal mode of operation when the Emergency mode is turned off.

- o To turn off the emergency mode, select ⋮ More options and click Turn off Emergency mode.

CHAPTER THREE
CAMERA AND GALLERY

The Camera and the Gallery app work together in the sense that picture and video that are taken by the camera can be viewed and edited in the Gallery.

Camera

Use the camera app to capture images and record videos.

- From the Apps screen or the Home screen select the ⌾ Camera app icon.

TIP: While the screen is off, press the Side key twice quickly to activate the camera.

Navigate the camera screen

Use the front and rear camera of your gadget to capture vibrant images.

1. Launch the 📷 Camera app and use the following options to set up your shots:
   - Choose a part to focus your camera on.
   - Touch the screen for a brightness scale to appear, then drag the brightness scale slowly to adjust the screen brightness.

- On the camera screen to switch between the front and rear camera.
- To zoom to an exact level touch 1x and touch an option at the bottom part of your screen.
- Swipe on your screen to the left or right to use another shooting mode.
- Click on the icon for ⚙ Settings to alter the settings of the camera.

2. Click on the icon for ◯ Capture to take an image.

Configure shooting mode

Leave the decision of choosing an ideal shooting mode to the camera or select the shooting mode you prefer.

- o To change the shooting mode on your camera, swipe left or right on the 📷 Camera app.
- Fun: Use the unique Snapchat lenses to customize your look.
- Portrait: For portrait image, change the background of your shots.

- Photo: Choose a picture setting with the help of your camera.
- Video: Choose a video setting with the help of your camera.
- More: Choose from available shooting modes. While at the lower part of the camera screen, click ⊕ to add and take away mode from the shooting modes tray.
  - Pro: When capturing photos, you can manually adjust the white balance, color tone and exposure value.
  - Pro video: When recording in Pro mode, you can modify the color tone, exposure value and white balance.
  - Single take: Capturing different pictures and video clip from different angles can be done when using Single take mode.
  - Panorama: Using either a horizontal or vertical camera, capture pictures to create a linear image.

- Night: In absence of the device's flash, images can be taken in low light conditions.
- Food: Capture images with more emphasis on the color of food.
- Macro: Capture pictures that you are about 3-5 centimeters away from you.
- Super slow-mo: To watch video in high quality slow motion, record them at a super high frame rate.
- Slow motion: To watch movies in slow motion, record them at a super high frame rate.
- Hyperlapse: Record footage at different frame rates, so that you can create a time lapse video.

AR Zone

The following should be done to access all the features of the augmented reality in one place.

- o To access the AR zone features, launch the device's Camera application and select More, then tap AR Zone.
  - AR Emoji Studio: You Emoji avatar can be created in the menu.

- AR Emoji Camera: From this menu, you can create your own Emoji avatar too.
- AR Emoji Stickers: Stickers can be added to your Emoji avatar from here.
- AR Doodle: Write on your video to enhance their quality.
- Deco Pic: Decorate your images.

Single take

An AI is being used by this shooting mode to create a high-quality image and video from different angles.

1. Select the Single take option under More in the ◉ Camera app.
2. Move around the scene to capture multiple angles and views after clicking on the ◯ Record icon.
- Go to the Gallery app where you will be able to view all your pictures captures and videos recorded.

Record videos

Using the device's camera can also enable you to record smooth and natural lifelike videos on your phone.

1. Enter the Camera screen and swipe to the left or right till you see Video.
2. To begin the process, simply tap the button for Record.
   - While recording is going on you can capture some images by tapping the Capture icon.
   - To take a break while recording, select the Pause icon, then select the Resume icon to continue from where you stopped in the recording.
3. When you are done with the recording process you can simply press the Stop icon too end the recording.

Camera settings

Personalize the settings that came along with your camera

- To customize your camera settings, select ⚙ Settings in the 📷 Camera app.

Intelligent features

- Scene optimizer: Set the camera to adjust the color settings of your images automatically.
- Shot suggestions: Get suggestions for lining up great shots.
- Scan QR codes: Set the camera to detect a QR code automatically while using it.

Pictures

- Swiping Shutter button: You will have the access to choose between burst shots or even create your own GIF, by swiping the shutter button to the nearest edge of the screen.
- High efficiency pictures: To save your storage space, store images in the HEIF format.

Although this format is not accepted by all sharing sites.

Selfies

- Save selfies as previewed: Store selfies as they are displayed.

Videos

- Auto FPS: Automatically optimize the frame rate in video mode so that you can record brighter videos in low-light conditions.
- Video steadiness: Turn on the feature "Anti-Shake" so that you can keep focus while the camera is in motion.
- Decrease the sizes of files: Saving videos in the HEVC format is advisable for conservation of space. The format is not also supported by all sharing sites.

General

- Auto HDR: More information can be captured in some bright or dark areas of your shots.
- Grid lines: Turn on the viewfinder gridlines to help in composing your image or video.

- Location tags: Include a GPS location tag to your image or video.
- Shooting patterns:
  - You can capture an image, zoom to a precise level, control the volume level and also record a video by pressing the volume button.
  - Use a voice command to capture a picture.
  - Upload an optional shutter button that can be taken anywhere on the screen.
  - Your picture will be taken in few seconds just by showing your palm to the camera.
- Settings to reserve: Select to either to launch the Camera screen with the same shooting mode.
- Storage location: Select your desired storage location to store your images or videos.
  - An external memory card needs to be installed to view storage location.
- Watermark: This can be added at the bottom part of your image.
- Shutter sound: Produce a capturing sound.

- Show Snapchat Lenses in Fun mode: Turn this feature on to include Snapchat filters to Fun mode.
- Privacy Notice: view the info of the camera privacy.
- Permissions: Check the required permission for the Camera.
- Reset settings: Select this option to return the camera to its default settings automatically.
- About Camera: View the software version and app info.

GALLERY

The Galley app on your device is useful in viewing and editing all your captured pictures and recorded videos.

- Select the ✪ Gallery app on the Apps list.

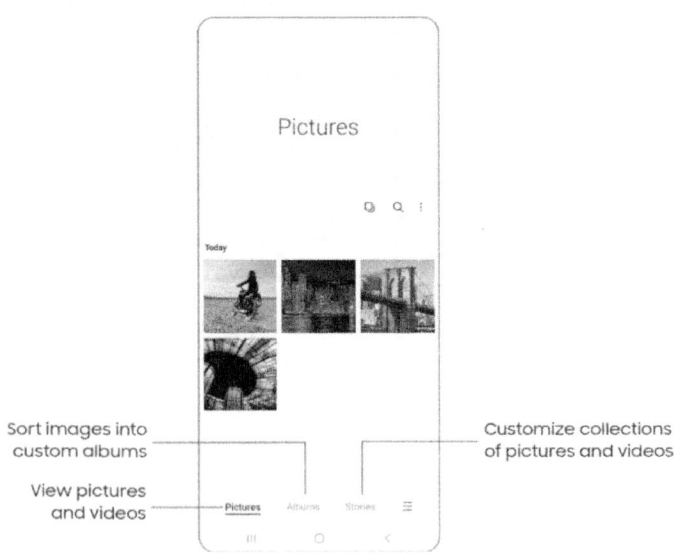

View pictures

1. From Apps click on ✪ Gallery then select the Pictures menu.
2. Tap a picture or video to launch it. Slide to the left or right on the gallery screen to launch other videos or photos.

- To initiate the Bixby usage, press  .
- Select ♡ to add picture to Favorites.
- Select ⋮ More to see the following features:
- Details: View the image information.
- Re-master picture: Use automatic image to enhance a picture.
- Add portrait effect: Move the slider to decrease the portrait picture background visibility.
- Copy to clipboard: Copy your image to the clipboard so that you can past it in another application.
- Set as wallpaper: Make the image your background image.
- Move to Secure Folder: Move your images to the secure folder.
- Print: Print pictures out from your smart phone.

Edit pictures

Use the editing tools of the gallery app to edit your images.

1. Enter the ✹ Gallery application and select Pictures.
2. For further option on the image that you have selected, click ✎ Edit:

- ✴ Auto adjusts: This feature will auto improve the image.

- ⬜ Transform: This tool can help you to rotate, flip and crop the image.

- ⊗ Filters: Enhance the color of your picture.

- ☼ Tone: Enhance the brightness, contract and other settings of the background.

- ☺ Decorations: Upload sticker or emoji to beautify your pictures.

- ⋮ More options: Select this to view other editing options.

- Revert: All changes applied to the picture can be undone with this tool.
3. When you are done with the editing click Save.

Play video

Play the saved videos in your Gallery application.

1. Select the "Video" menu in the ✽ Gallery app.
2. Swipe to the left or right on the Gallery screen to watch other videos.

- Click ♡ to add video to Favorites. Move to the bottom part of the screen to view the favorite album.

- Click ⋮ More to see more features:
- Details: View the video information and edit them.
- Launch in Video player: Play the video in the default player of video.
- Set as wallpaper: Make the video your desktop background.
- Move to Secure Folder: Move your videos to the secure folder.

3. To launch the video, select ▶ Play.

Share pictures and videos

You have access to sharing your videos and pictures to family and friends from within the Gallery app.

1. From the ✳ Gallery app select Pictures or Videos.
2. Select the picture or video that you want to share from the menu that appears after clicking ⋮ More options and Edit.
3. Choose the app you want to use in sharing from the menu that appear when you click ⤳ Share.

Delete pictures and videos

All or some of your pictures and video can be deleted from your device through the Gallery app.

1. From ✳ Gallery, select Edit under ⋮ More options.
2. Press the image and videos you want to remove from your device.

3. Hit the 🗑 Delete icon.

Group similar images

Sort images by their similarities in the Gallery app

1. Choose the 🗇 Group similar images icon on the ✻ Gallery app.

2. To return all the comparable images to their default manner select 🗇 Ungroup similar images.

TAKE A SCREENSHOT

Take an image of what is currently going on in your screen, the screenshot folder will be created in your Gallery app automatically.

- o At the same time, the Side key and Volume downward key should be pressed and released after the image has been captured.

Palm swipe to capture a screenshot

Swipe the edge of your hand across an image from side to side remaining in contact with the screen to capture a screenshot.

1. From the device Settings app, select ⊙ Advanced features and click Motions and gestures then Palm swipe to capture.

2. This feature will be turned on immediately you tap ⬤.

Screenshot settings

Change the settings for your screenshot.

- To alter the screenshot settings, launch the ⊙ Advanced features menu in the Setting app and select Screenshots and screen recorder.

  - Screenshot toolbar: Display additional options after capturing the images of your screen.

  - Don't show the status and navigation bars: Refuse to display the status and navigation bar in your screenshots.

  - Delete shared screenshots: Auto delete shared screenshots.

- Screenshot saving format: Your screenshot can be saved as a JPEG or PNG format depending on your choice.

SCREEN RECORDER

You can record footage of what is happening on your screen.

1. To do this, launch the Screen recorder menu in the Quick setting panel.
2. Select how you want the sound the select Start recording.
3. Before the recording will kick start, a three second countdown will run on the screen. You can also skip the countdown to begin the recording automatically.

- To draw on the video that you are recording, click Draw.
- If you want to record video with the camera, Click Selfie video.

4. The process of the screen recording will end when you tap Stop.

Screen recorder settings

All your screen recorder settings can be modified from this menu.

- o To do this, select Screenshot and Screen recorder in the ⚙ Advanced feature menu under Settings.
  - Sound: Choose the sound that you want to use in the recording.
  - Video quality: Choose a resolution for your video.
  - Selfie video size: Adjust the size of the video.
  - Display touches: Turn this on, so that all tap made on the screen will appear on the recording.

CHAPTER FOUR
APPLICATIONS

All applications both default and downloaded are all displayed in the Apps list.

- o To access the Apps list of your device, swipe upward from the Home screen.

Uninstall or disable apps

Apps you don't want on your gadget can be either disabled or uninstalled. Apps that are disabled cannot be seen in the Apps list, default apps can only disable and can't be uninstalled.

- o From the Apps list, press and hold an application then then select Uninstall or Disable.

Search for apps

Use this feature to look for apps that are not displayed in the Apps list.

1. Click on the Search bar in the Apps list. Apps and settings that tallies with your search input will appear on the screen as a result.
2. Touch a result to launch it.

TIP: Select the ⋮ More options icon then Settings to modify the search settings.

Sort apps

Edit how you want the arrangement of apps to be in the Apps list.

- o The option to arrange the apps in the Apps list will appear when you tap ⋮ More options > tap Sort:
  - Your own order: To arrange apps in your own manner touch the Custom order.
  - Alphabetical order: Apps will be arranged alphabetically when you touch this.

NOTE: You can remove empty icon spaces by touching ⋮ More options then Clean up pages, if you arrange apps manually.

Create and use folders

Apps shortcut are easily arranged on the Apps list with the folders.

1. Press and hold an app icon then move it on top of another app

2. Release the app on top of the other to create the folder.

- Folder name: Create a name for your new folder.

- ◯ Palette: Change the color of the folder to make them identifiable from each other.

- ✛ Add apps: Pick and add apps to the created folder.

3. To leave the folder, touch ❮.

Copy a folder to a Home screen

Copy a folder from the Apps list to add it to the Home screen.

o Press and hold the folder from the Apps list the pick ⌂ Add to Home.

Delete a folder

All apps in a folder will return to the Apps list if the folder is deleted.

1. To delete a folder, launch the Apps list and press and hold a folder you want to delete.

2. Click the 🗑 Delete icon that will appear when holding the folder icon to delete the folder.

Game Booster

Get more improved performance on a game you are playing. While gaming, you can block all call and notifications.

- o To view the navigation bar while gaming, swipe from the bottom of your screen upward. On the right and left sides, you will see the following:

  - Touch protection: Put a lock on the screen to prevent unintentional touch.

  - Game Booster: Other options like, blocking the navigation bar, screenshot and screen touches can be customized.

App settings

Customize all your device app settings.

- o Launch Settings Apps and then click Apps. Click any of the option to customize:

- Choose default apps: Pick an application to be used for making of calls, sending text and more.
- Samsung app settings: View the Samsung apps list and change their settings.
- Your apps: To update the info about an app and its privacy or usage setting, touch the app icon.

TIP: To reset all app settings click on the More options icon and select the Reset app preferences button.

SAMSUNG APPLICATIONS

The apps that are show on the list below may either be downloaded or available on your device by default during setup.

AR Zone

From one place all the Augmented reality feature can be accessed from one place when using this app.

Bixby

This feature reads and gets used to your routine then suggest contents that you may be interested in.

Galaxy Store

From the Galaxy store you can get apps and other packages that are customize to the use of Samsung devices.

Galaxy Wearable

You can use this feature to create a connection between your device and a Galaxy watch

Game Launcher

This feature arranges all your apps in one place automatically.

NOTE: To turn on the Game launcher from the Settings if it is not seen in the Apps list, click on the ⚙ Advanced feature menu and tap Game launch and finally, tap ⬤.

Samsung Free

This feature offers you free access to watch live TV shows, new and other exclusive contents.

Samsung Global Goals

Under this menu you can learn more details about the Global Goals initiative and contribute towards donations that support these causes with ads.

Samsung TV Plus

You can enjoy some entertainments like, news, sport and many more on your phone, free of charge.

SmartThings

You can use the Smart Thins app to connect different device at the same time. With this app you can also control or monitor your environment through your phone to suit your needs. Look at the dashboard of this app to view the status of your device.

Tips

Some tips and patterns like user manual of your phone are revealed to you.

CALCULATOR

Some basic and essential mathematical calculations can be carried out with this feature. The unit converter and the scientific math functions is also available.

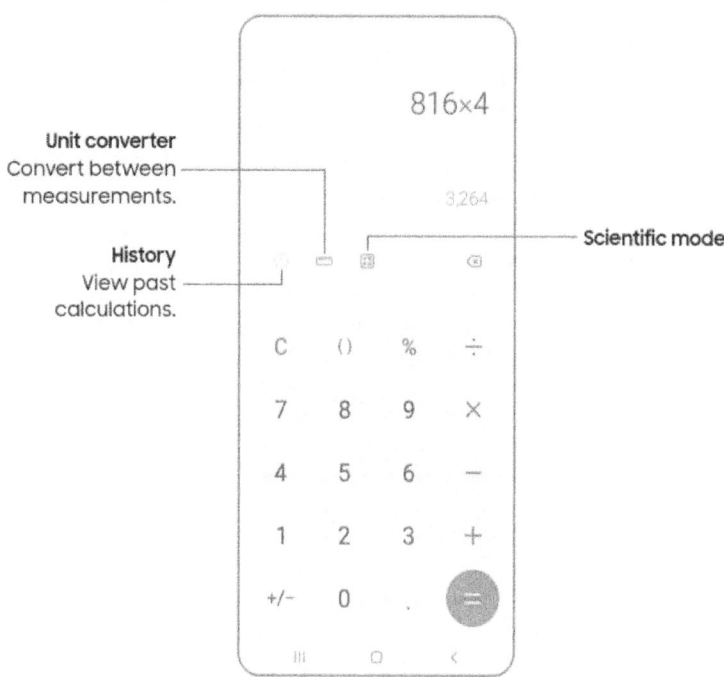

CALENDAR

From this app, you can keep track of the exact date of the month or year, you can also connect the app to various account opened online to consolidate all calendars in one position.

Add calendars

1. To add a calendar, launch the Calendar app and select the Navigation drawer button.

2. Select the Manage calendars menu then tap Add account then choose the account type to add the account.

3. Manually input the details of the account and follow the easy steps.

TIP: The account that you have added to your calendar app may support email, contacts and more.

Calendar alert style

You can set alert style for the calendar app.

1. Open the 🗓 Calendar apps and select ⚙ Calendar settings under the ≡ Navigation drawer the select Alert style to configure the alert style for your calendar.
2. The following options are seen:
- Light: Produce a little sound when notifications are received.
- Medium: Produce a little sound when you receive a full screen notification.
- Strong: Get a notification on the full screen and play a sound until the notification is dismissed.
3. You will see the following options based on the alert style you select

- Short sound: Select the short sound for Light or Medium styles.
- Long sound: Choose the long sound for strong alert style.

Create an event

1. To create an event, open the 🗓 Calendar app and touch the ⊕ icon to add an event.
2. Enter the even information manually and tap Save to create the event.

Delete an event

Follow instruction to delete an event from your Calendar.

1. To delete an event that you created, open the 🗓 Calendar app and select the event you want to delete.
2. Touch the event again to edit it
3. To delete the event fully, press the 🗑 icon.

CLOCK

Set up alarms and monitor the time.

Alarm

To set an alarm to play once or every day, do the following.

1. After launching the ⏰ Clock application, select the Alarm tab and select ＋ Add alarm.
2. Do the following to set up the alarm:
- Time: Choose the time that you want the alarm to play.

- Day: Pick a day from the list of the days of the week that the alarm should play.
- Alarm name: Type in the name of the alarm on the input field manually for easy identification.
- Alarm sound: Choose from the default alarm tones or select from your device audio, then drag the slider the setup the alarm volume level.
- Vibration: You can turn on this feature if you want your alarm to vibrate.
- Snooze: Allow sleeping. Configure the alarm to play again within a certain period of time.
3. To save the alarm that you have created, select the Save option.

TIP: Kindly hit the ⋮ More options button and tap bedtime and wake up time to add your sleeping routines or create a bedtime notice.

Delete an alarm

To delete an alarm from your device, do the following:

1. Press and hold the alarm that you want to delete in the ⊙ Clock application.
2. After pressing and holding the alarm for a certain period, press 🗑 Delete.

Alert settings

You can make your gadget vibrate for all notifications and alerts.

1. Select Settings under ⋮ More options in the ⊙ Clock application menu.
2. To turn on this feature, hit Vibrate for alarm and timers.

WORLD CLOCK

You will be able to monitor time in different time zones and cities.

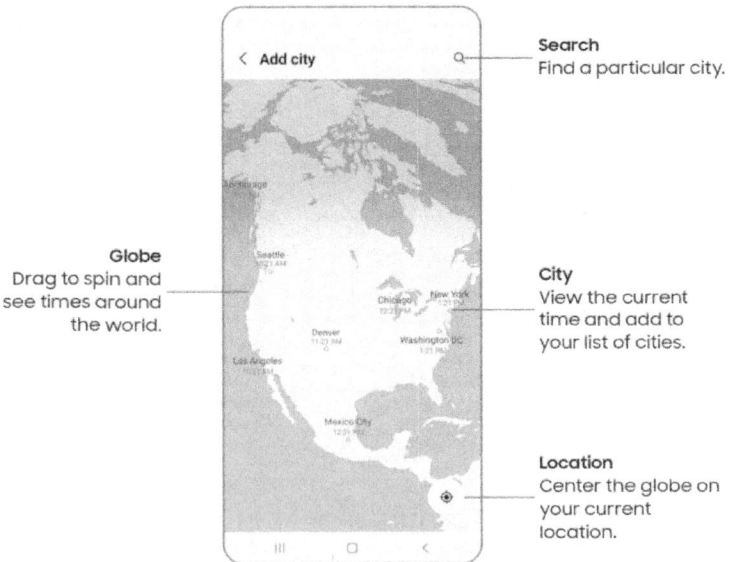

1. From ⊙ Clock select World clock.
2. Select ＋ Add city.
3. To add your desired city, spin the globe until the city you want to add appears then tap Add.
   - Press and hold a city you want to delete and tap 🗑 .

Time zone converter

With the time zone converter, you can check the time in a city and also tell what that time will be in another city.

1. From ⓐ Clock select World clock.

2. Select ⋮ More and hit Time zone converter.

3. To choose another city, hit ▼ Menu.

- To add a city from the menu list hit ✚.

4. Swipe the Hours, Minutes, Seconds or Periods (AM or PM) to set the time.

- The clock app menu will return to its default settings when your hit the Reset button.

Weather settings

To change the settings of your weather, follow the instructions on the clock app under World clock.

1. Select the World clock menu under the ⓐ Clock application.

2. To turn the weather settings on or off, tap the ⋮More options icon and select Settings the Show weather information
3. To change the temperature form Celsius to Fahrenheit, click Temperature.

Stopwatch

Use the stop watch feature to time events that are taking place for up to a hundredth of seconds. To use the stop watch, do the following:

1. Select the Stop watch menu in the ⏱ Clock app.
2. To turn on the timer click Start.
- To keep the track of time, select Lap.
3. The process will pause when you tap Stop and resume when you tap Resume.
- Select the Reset option to take the Stopwatch back to zero.

Timer

To initiate a countdown process, tag along side with the instructions below.

1. Select the "Timer" option in the 🅞 Clock app
2. To set the timer, use the keypad to enter the Hours, Minutes, and seconds as you prefer.
3. To initiate the process, select Start.
- To put the timer to a temporary pause select Stop and tap Resume to begin from where you stopped.
- To stop the timer and reset it click Cancel.

Preset timer

To allocate a name or save your fixed timer, tag along side with the below instructions.

1. From the 🅞 Clock app, select ➕ Add preset timer under the "Timer" option.
2. You can also change the name and countdown time for the timer.
3. To save the timer you have created, select the option "Add".

- To change the settings of your preset timer, take the following actions;

  - Select More >Edit preset timers.

Timer options

Follow instruction below to customize the Timer options.

1. From Clock app, click Timer.
2. Select the More options icon and tap Settings.

- Sound: From the menu that appears after you tap Settings you can choose a default sound or add you own.
- Vibration: You can turn vibration for the timer on.
- Display mini timer: Turn this on to show a pop-up window of the timer if you minimize the clock app.

General settings

Everything about the clock app is detail in the sections of the manual.

- o To access them, go to the ⓐ Clock app and choose the "Settings" option under ⋮ More.
- Customization Service: Sign in to your Samsung account to enable you customize private or personal content.
- About Clock: View the software version and recent updates.

CHAPTER FIVE
CONTACTS

From the Contacts application you can view and manage all your contacts. You can also add your contacts to your personal email accounts.

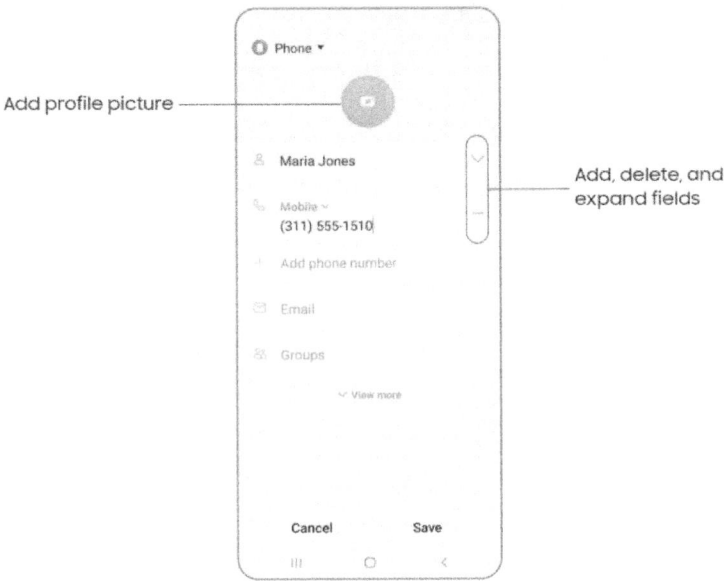

Create a contact

1. For contact creation, launch the contacts application and select Create contact.
2. Enter the contact details manually and select Save.

Edit a contact

To change a contact and its appearance, follow the steps below. Contacts info can be changed and deleted.

1. To edit a contact, launch the 👤 Contacts application and select the contact you want to edit.

2. Click the ✏ Edit icon to change the contact information.

3. Tap any of the contact field to either change, add or delete contact information.

4. Select the option for Save.

Favorites

Favorite contacts can be accessed from other apps as they are listed on top of the contact list on your Contacts application.

1. To add a contact as favorite, launch the 👤 Contacts app and choose the contact that you want to add to the favorite list.

2. Select the ☆ Star icon to add the contact to your favorites.

- Select the ★ Yellow star icon on the contact that you want to remove from the favorite list to remove it.

Share a contact

Contacts on the Contact apps can be shared with other apps and services.

1. To share a contact from the 👤 Contact app, touch the contact.
2. Select the ⤴ Share option.
3. You can choose a method to share the contact as, either as a file or text.
4. Choose the method you want to use to share the contact and follow the prompts.

TIP: To share the contact by scanning a QR code, select the ⋮ More options icon and select QR code.

GROUPS

All your contacts are sorted properly with the help of a group.

Create a group

1. The first step to take towards creating a group is, opening the ● Contacts app

2. After opening the contacts app select the ≡ Show navigation menu and select Groups.

3. To create the group, click create and input the group details manually:

- Group name: Choose a name you want the group to be identified as.
- Group ringtone: Choose a ringtone to play for the group.
- Add member: Add members to the group you have created.

4. Select the Save option.

Add or remove group contacts

Contacts can be added to the group or removed.

- o To remove contacts or add them to the group, go to the 👤 Contacts, select ≡ Show navigation menu and tap Groups and choose a group that you want to add contacts to or remove contacts from.

- Press and hold the contact you want to delete from the groups to mark it then press 🗑 Delete.

- Press the ✎ Edit icon on the Group menu and select Add members then choose the contact you want to add and select Done.

Send a message to a group

Do the following to send a message to a group:

1. Select the groups you want to send a message to on the Groups menu under the ≡ Show navigation menu in the 👤 Contacts app.
2. Select More and tap Send message.

Send an email to a group

Do the following to email a group.

1. Select a group under the Groups menu under ☰ Show navigation menu in the 👤 contacts app.

2. Choose Send email after tapping ⋮ More options.

3. Choose the contacts in the group that you want to send the email to or click on the Check box to mark all the contacts in the group and click Done.

   NOTE: You will only see group members with email address on their contact info.

4. Select an email to send and follow the instructions.

Delete a group

To delete a group

1. Launch the application for 👤 Contacts, select ☰ Show navigation menu and finally tap Groups, and choose a group.

2. Click the ⋮ More options icon and click Delete.
- Select Remove group only if it is only the group you want to delete.
- Select Remove group and move members to trash if it is the group and the contacts in it you want to delete.

Merge contacts

To merge contacts.

1. Launch the app "👤 Contacts", click ☰ Show navigation and tap Manage contacts.
2. All contacts with double emails, phone numbers and name will be joined together when you tap Merge.
3. Choose the contacts that appear and select Merge.

Import contacts

To import contacts.

1. Launch the 👤 Contacts application on your device and select the ☰ Show navigation menu and select Manage contacts.

2. Select Import contacts and follow the instructions.

Export contacts

To export contacts.

1. Launch the Contacts application on your device and select the ☰ Show navigation menu then Manage contacts.
2. Select Export contact and follow the instructions.

Sync contacts

To sync contact to your cloud accounts

1. Launch the Contacts application on your device and select the ☰ Show navigation menu and select Manage contacts.
2. Select Sync contacts.

Delete contacts

To eliminate a contact from your list of contacts

1. Press and hold the contact you want to delete in the 👤 Contacts app.

2. Select the 🗑 Delete icon and confirm when prompted.

CHAPTER SIX
INTERNET

This feature is a well recommended browser that is reliable and fast for your Smartphone. Other features like the Secret mode browsing and the Biometric Web Login are also available in the app.

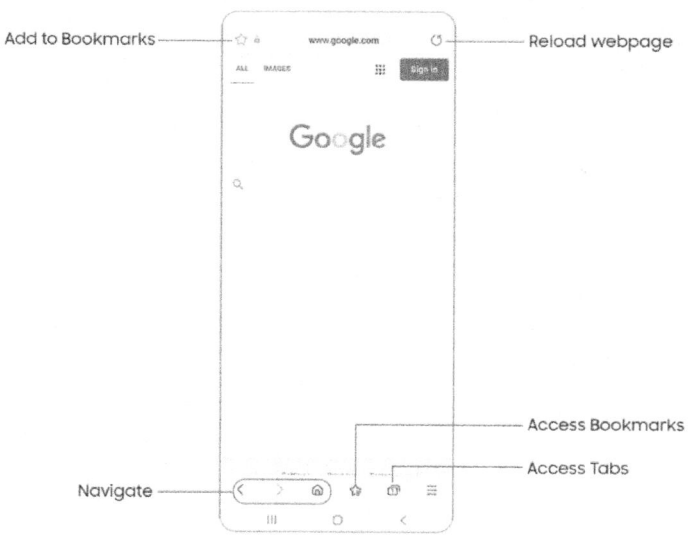

Browser tabs

You can access multiple web pages at the same time under the menu.

- Launch the application ⬤ Internet and touch 1️⃣ Tabs > New tab.

- To close the tab that is recently opened, select  Tabs and ⊗ Close tab.

Create a Bookmark

When a web page is bookmarked, it can be easily accessed in the Internet app.

- o Press the ☆ Star icon on the ◯ Internet app to create a Bookmark.

Open a Bookmark

To open a bookmarked page

1. Go to the ◯ Internet app and select ☆ Bookmarks.
2. Choose an entry of bookmark.

Save a web page

To save a page

- o Go to the ◯ Internet app a click ≡ Tools then tap Add page.
  - Bookmarks: Add the page to your list of bookmarks.

- Quick access: View a frequently accessed or saved web page.
- Home screen: Add the Web page to home screen menu.
- Saved pages: Save the content of the web page on your gadget so that it can be accessed later while you are offline.

View history

To view all the web pages that you have visited.

- Select History under the ☰ Tools menu in the ◯ Internet app.

TIP: Select Clear history under ⋮ More options to delete the browsing history form your device.

Share pages

To share pages that you have accessed with your contacts.

- On the ◯ Internet app, select ☰ Tools and hit share.

SECRET MODE

If any page is accessed from the Secret mode, it will not be listed on your browser history or search history. The Secret mode tab is darker than the regular browsing tab.

- On the ⬤ Internet program, select ⬜1 Tabs and click on Turn on secret mode.

Secret mode settings

To change the settings of your Secret mode

1. From the ⬤ Internet, click ⬜1 Tabs to add new tab.

2. Select ⋮ More options and click Secret mode settings.

- Make use of the password: You are required to set a new password to use secret mode.

- Use the Face verification: The face verifications process can also be used to keep this feature private.

- Validation of Fingerprints: The fingerprint validation process can also keep this feature private.
- Reset Secret mode: All secret mode data can be cleared from this menu and return to the regular browsing mode.

Turn off secret mode

To turn off the secret mode and return to your regular browsing, do the following:

- To disable the secret mode from the ⬤ Internet app, select 1⃣ Tabs and click Turn off secret mode.

Internet settings

To customize the Internet app settings

- Select the ☰ Tools menu and hit Settings in the ⬤ Internet app.

MESSAGES

From this app, you can share text, images, videos and emojis to your friends and loved ones across the globe.

o To start a conversation, select the Compose icon on the Messages app.

Message search

Look for a particular message in the Message app.

1. Select the icon for Search in the Messages app.

2. Use the keyboard to enter the search inputs manually and hit 🔍 Search.

Delete conversations

To remove the history of conversations in the Messages app, do the following.

1. Click the ⋮ More options icon in the Messages app and tap Delete.
2. Press and hold the chats that you want to delete to select them.
3. After touching the conversation, press the 🗑 Delete icon.

Send SOS messages

To send an SOS message when you are in an emergency state, do the following.

1. Launch the app called Settings on your gadget and select the 🆘 Safety and emergency icon then tap Send SOS messages, and toggle the feature on by tapping ⬤ .

- You can set your gadget to send the SOS message when the Side Button is pressed either 3 or 4 times depending on how you want it.
- Click Auto call someone to choose a contact that you trust that you want to call immediately after sending the SOS message.
- Click attach photo to include an image to the emergency message.
- Select Attach audio recording to add a recording of five seconds to your SOS message.
- Select Send message to, if you wish to add a receiver by creating new contacts or selecting from your Contacts.

2. To send the message, press the side key three of four times, based on your choice.

Message settings

Change the Settings for your Messages app.

- o Hit the ⋮ More options symbol in the 💬 Messages app and select Settings.

Emergency alerts

Enable this feature, so that you can be notified about threat and other situations. No charge is applied to getting an emergency alert.

- o To change the settings for emergency alerts, launch the Settings application and click on 🔒 Safety and emergency then hit Wireless Emergency Alerts.

TIP: From the Notification menu you can launch the Emergency alerts. To do this, Launch the Settings app and click 🔔 Notification then Advanced settings and click on Wireless emergency alerts.

MY FILES

From this application, you can view all your device media (Images, Videos, Audio and Documents). File that are stored on your SD card and Cloud accounts can also be viewed if supported.

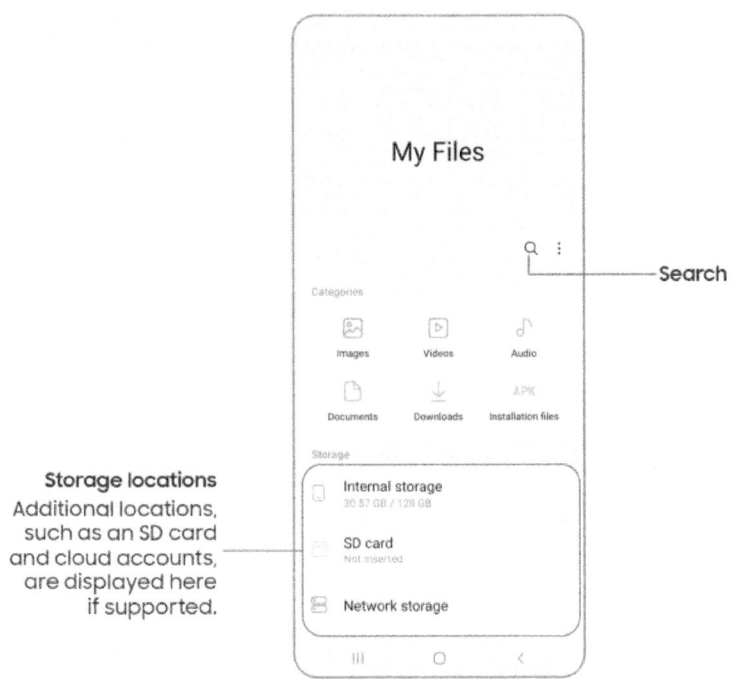

File groups

All the files that are embedded on your device are arranged in the following folders:

- Recent files: See files that have been viewed not too long.

- You will only see this if you have launched more than one file.
- Categories: All files will appear depending on their type.
- Storage: See the SD card or your Cloud accounts.
- The account on Cloud varies depending on the kind of service you log in to.
- Evaluate Storage: View what's eating up your device space.

My Files settings

Change the My file settings and all the file in it.

o To change the Settings for the My Files app, go to the ⬜ app and select ⋮ More options and tap settings

- Cloud accounts: Connect to and manage your gadget cloud services.
- File management: Manage how file appears, how they are deleted, and how they access mobile data.

- Examine storage: See what is eating up your storage space.
- Privacy: View the permission for My Files app.

CHAPTER SEVEN
PHONE

More can be done on the Phone app other than just making phone calls.

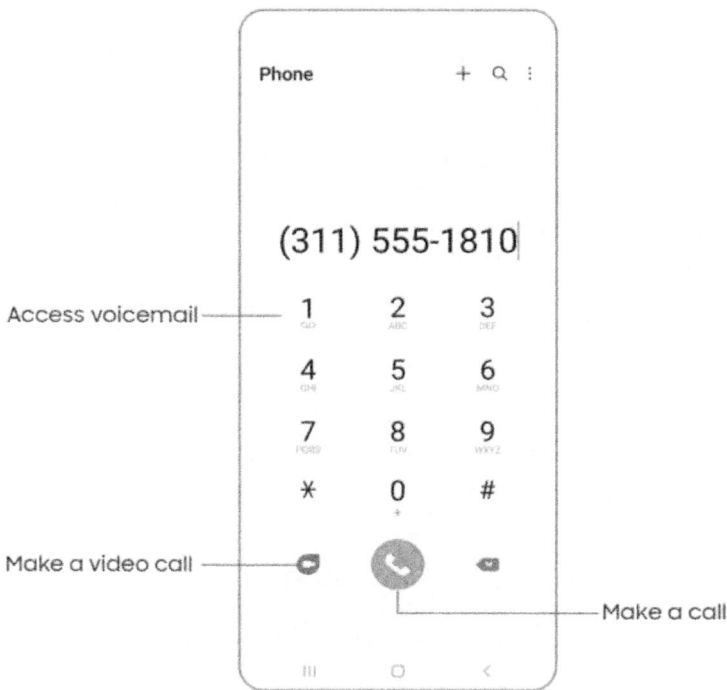

Calls

From the Phone app, you can make and receive a call. You can also view all the recent calls, dialed calls, missed calls and favorite contacts.

Make a call

To make a call

- Launch the Phone application and select the Call icon.

Make a call from Recent

A call can be made from your list of recent calls on your call history.

1. Launch the Phone software and select Recent to show a list of all your recent calls.
2. Choose the contact that you want to call and hit Call the contact.

Make a call from Contacts

You can make a call from the Contacts application.

- To make a call from the app, launch it by tapping its icon and swipe your finger across a number to the right to call the contact.

Answer a call

Your device will ring and the name of the caller or the phone number of the caller will appear on the pop-up screen for an incoming call.

- o To answer the incoming call, you will see the ☎ Answer icon on the screen, drag it to the right.

Decline a call

To decline a call

- o To decline an incoming call, you will see the ⌒ Decline icon on the screen, drag it to the left.

Decline with a message

To decline a call using a message

- o On the incoming call screen, drag upward the Send message menu and select a message to send.

End a call

- o When you are done talking, and you want to end the call, click ⌒.

Actions while on a call

You can perform many actions while on a call, these actions include; Adjusting the call volume, switching to a headset or speaker, or even multitask.

- o Use the phone's volume key to adjust the volume.

Switch to headset or speaker

To switch to another means of listening to the call.

- To hear the caller on your phone's speaker, select 🔊.

- To hear the caller on an external Bluetooth device, select ✶.

Multitask

Other apps can be used while you are still making a call. Once the active call screen is minimized the call will appear on the Status bar of the device.

To return to the call screen:

- o Draw down the status bar top show the notification panel and tap the call on the notification panel.

To end a call while multitasking:

- To end the call while you are multitasking, drag the status bar downward to show the notification panel and click .

Call background

Choose an image that will appear on the ongoing call screen.

- To select a call background, go to the Phone app and select click More > tap Settings then select Call background for the options listed below:
  - Layout: Decide how the info of the caller will appear if the caller has a profile photo.
  - Background: While making a call, choose a picture to appear.

Call pop-up settings

Calls will appear as a small pop-up on your screen, if another app is on use.

- To set this, go to the Phone app, click More > press Settings and select Call display while using applications to use the following options:

- Full screen: Turn this on for the incoming call to appear on the full screen preview.
- Pop-up: Turn this feature on for call to appear as a pop-up at the top of your screen.
- Mini pop-up: Activate this for calls to appear as a small pop-up on your screen.
- Keep calls in pop-up: Once this feature is activated, all calls will remain in the pop-up menu even after they are answered.

Manage calls

All calls including the missed, dialed and received calls are stored in the call log. From this menu, numbers can be blocked, speed dials can be set and also you can use voicemail.

Call log

o Select Recent top view a list of recent calls in the 🅲 Phone app.

Save a contact from a recent call

1. To save a contact, launch the Phone app and select the Recent button then choose the contact that you want to save.
2. Touch the call that has the details that you want to save and select Add to contacts.
3. Depending on your device preference, you may see Create new contact or Update existing contact.

Delete call records

1. To erase your call log, launch the Phone application and select Recent.
2. Press and hold the contact that you want to remove from the call log.
3. Select 🗑.

Block a number

You can add number to your block list, of which they cannot be able to reach you, but their calls will be sent directly to voicemail.

1. To add a number to your block list, open the app of the 📞 Phone and click Recent.
2. Choose the contact that you want to add to the block list and tap ⓘ Details.
3. To block the contact, select 🚫 Block or tap the ⋮ More options button and select Block contact.

Emergency calls

Without an activated service on your gadget you can still make emergency calls.

1. To make an emergency call, launch the 📞 Phone software on your gadget then enter the details of the emergency number that you want to call and select "Call".

TIP: Even while you are on the lock screen emergency can still be made, which helps people that don't have access to your device to call for help in an emergency mode.

Phone settings

Change the settings of the Phone application.

- o To change the settings of the 🅒 Phone app, launch the app and select the ⋮ More options button and press Settings.

Place a multi-party call

To place a multiparty call, do the following:

1. To the active call screen, select the ➕ Plus icon to add another contact.

2. Select the new contact and select 📞 Call.

3. If the second call is answered, do the following:

- 🔄 Swap: Click this icon to switch between the two calls.

- ↠ Merge: Click this icon to merge both calls together.

Video calls

To make video calls on your gadget:

- Go to the default 📞 Phone application and select the number you want to make a video contact with and select either of 🎥 Video call, 📹 Meet or 📷 Video call.

TIP: This feature is not supported by all gadgets.

SAMSUNG HEALTH

This feature assists in monitoring your daily usage such as your diet, sleep and more.

TIP: Your gadget will not use all the information, provided by Samsung health or related software for treatment or diagnosis.

Environmental factors and specific activity performed while using or wearing or the device may affect the correctness of data provided by this Samsung health and its related software.

Before you start exercising

It is best that you see a physician before you begin an exercise routine even though the Samsung Health apps is a companion to your routine of exercise, you can do physical activities such as brisk walking that is safe for majority of people. If you are passing through any of these conditions listed below, see a doctor before embarking on any exercise routine:

- Muscle pain
- Heart disease

- Arthritis
- Pain in the Chest, jaw and arm region
- Ankle swelling most especially at night
- Breath shortness
- Asthma and lung disease
- Diabetes
- Dizziness or loss of consciousness
- Liver or kidney disease
- Rapid heartbeat

If you are also pregnant, see the doctor before starting an exercise routine.

SAMSUNG NOTES

The Samsung Notes application, stores all the notes containing, voice recordings and music. Through social network service, you can quickly share and create notes.

To know more about this feature, visit the link below

Visitsamsung.com/us/support/owners/app/samsung-notes.

Create notes

1. To create note, go to the ⬜ Samsung Notes application and select ⬜ Add.
2. Create note with your device keypad.

Voice recordings

Follow steps below to add voice record to note.

1. To add a voice recording to your notes, click on the ⬜ Samsung Notes icon and tap ⬜ Add.
2. Select ⬜ Insert and touch Voice recording.
3. Use the text option to create/compose content.

Edit notes

1. To make changes to notes that you have already created, launch the ⬜ Samsung notes program and select the note that you want to make change to.
2. Select ⬜.

3. After finishing the editing process, select ◁ Navigate up to leave the menu.

Notes options

- From this menu you can perform a lot of activities, but first launch 🔲 Samsung Notes:
  - Import PDFs: Open a PDF file on Samsung Notes.
  - Search: Enter you search criteria and select search.
  - ⋮ More options:
    - Edit: Select from all notes the one to delete, save or share.
    - View: Pick from the Simple, Grid, or list view pattern.
    - Pin favorites to top: Mark favorite notes on top of your main page.

SAMSUNG PAY

You can make payment on your mobile phone with the Samsung Pay application. To use this app and feature, you will need to create a Samsung account.

NOTE: The Samsung Pay app does not store the details of your credit card on the cloud for the purpose of security. This app can be signed in to many devices.

- To use the application, launch the app by clicking its icon 🅿️ Samsung Pay then follow the screen prompts.

Use Samsung Pay

Launch the Samsung Pay application and hold your phone over the store card reader to use it.

1. Scan your fingerprint or enter the Samsung Pay PIN to choose a card to pay with the approve payments on the 🅿️ Samsung Pay app.

2. Hold your gadget to the back of the card reader.

- A debit receipt will be sent to registered email if the payment process is complete.

TIP: Make sure that you turn on the NFC feature on your gadget. For more information on this, see NFC and Payment.

Quick access

The Samsung Pay app can be opened from the Lock screen, Home screen or Off screen with the quick access.

1. Launch the Samsung Pay program and select Navigation drawer then tap Settings and select the Quick access option.

2. To turn on this feature, click .

To use Quick access:

1. Swipe up from the bottom of your screen to use the quick access.
   - This will display all your payment card and access.

2. Take the card down to leave Quick access.

Use gift cards with Samsung Pay

From an expanding selection of your favorite retailers, you can send, purchase, and redeem gift cards.

GOOGLE APPS

All apps that are show under this menu are all available on your gadget by default.

Chrome

This is a browsing site where you can source for more information, it can be used on smartphone and PC.

Drive

From this menu, you can back up your files to your cloud account so that you don't lose them when your gadget gets missing or stolen.

Duo

With the app you can initiate a video call across multiple devices and on the web.

Gmail

For more information on the Gmail feature click on the link below: support.google.com/mail.

Google

The Google app is also an exclusive app that can be used to look for recent update online.

Messages

You can create conversations with your contacts without an internet connection.

Photos

All the pictures that you have taken and videos that you have recorded are all stored in your Photos app when you can, share delete and edit them.

Play Store

The Google Play Store application is helpful to your device as it makes your device to have access to exclusive apps.

SETTINGS

Access Settings

You can access the Settings feature of your device in two ways.

- To launch it from the Home screen, swipe down to show the notifications center and tap ⚙ Settings.
- To launch the Settings menu from the apps list, click on ⚙ Settings.

Search for Settings

With the search feature you can find apps and feature that you are not sure of where to find them exactly.

1. Launch the Settings app and click the 🔍 Search icon and input your search criteria.
2. Tap an entry that appears to launch the settings.

Wi-Fi Connections

You can access the internet without using mobile data when you are connected to a W-Fi network.

1. To connect to a Wi-Fi and use the internet without data, go to the Settings app and select Connections then tap Wi-Fi

2. To activate the Wi-Fi feature, select the On icon and the device will scan for available networks.

3. Select a network from the list to connect to and enter the required password

    NOTE: Some Wi-Fi network don't need passcode.

4. Press the Connect button.

Connect to a hidden Wi-Fi network

The network you want to connect to sometimes may not be in the even after you have carried out a scan process. All you need to do is to connect to the Wi-Fi network manually by entering it details.

1. Go to the 📶 Connection menu in the Settings app and click Wi-Fi

2. Select ⬤.

3. Click on the ➕ Add button to add a network manually.

4. You will be asked to provide the following information:

- The name of the network will be needed from you.

- You will also need to choose the security option for the network and input the password if it is required.

- You can explore other advanced options, like IP and Proxy settings.

5. Hit the Save button to connect to the network.

TIP: Wi-Fi networks can be connected to simply by scanning their ▦ QR Code.

Wi-Fi Direct

This feature gives you access to share data between devices.

1. From the Settings app, click on the 🛜 Connection icon and select Wi-Fi.
2. Select the activation button ⬤.
3. Select Wi-Fi direct after clicking on the ⋮ More options button.
4. Choose the device that you want to connect to and follow the instructions.

Disconnect from Wi-Fi Direct

To disconnect from a Wi-Fi Direct.

1. From Settings, click on the 🛜 Connection button and tap Wi-Fi.
2. Select More options and press Wi-Fi Direct and select the device to disconnect from.

NFC AND PAYMENT

Communication with other devices without any network connection can be achieved with the help of this feature. This feature will not work if the device that you are transferring to doesn't support it. To use the feature both devices must be about four centimeters away from each other.

1. While on the Settings app select the Connection icon and select NFC and contactless payment.

2. Select to turn on the feature.

Tap and pay

Touch the back of your gadget to a compatible card reader to us the NFC payment application.

1. From the Settings menu, click Connections > NFC and contactless payments then click .

2. Select contactless payments to view the preloaded payment application.

- Click an app that is available to use it as a payment app.
- Select Pay with currently opened app to use the app that is opened currently to pay.
- Click others and select a service you prefer, to set another payment service as default.

DATA USAGE

From this menu you can check the level of your data usage. You can also set up limits.

o Launch the Settings app, select Data usage under Connections.

Turn on Data saver

The consumption of data on your device will be reduced if data saver is on, by preventing apps from sending and receiving data in background.

1. Enter the Settings app of your device and click Connections > Data usage and finally tap Data saver.
2. To activate this feature, select the activation button .

- While data saver is on and you want some apps to have unrestricted data usage, click allowed to use data while Date saver is on then touch next to each application to specify restrictions.

Monitor mobile data

Set limits and restrictions to control your mobile data access.

- o Launch the Settings application and select Connection and tap Data usage.

  You will see the following options:

- Mobile data: Use mobile data from your data plan.
- Mobile data only apps: Some apps can be allowed to use data even when your device is connected to Wi-Fi.
- Alert me about data usage: When your data reaches limit, set your device to alert you.
- Mobile data usage: You can view app usage of data.

- Billing cycle and data warning: Your monthly date can be set or changed to align you're your carrier's billing date.

Monitor Wi-Fi data

To monitor your Wi-Fi data

1. From the Settings app, click on Connections and finally select Data usage.
2. To check the usage of data over Wi-Fi connections over a period of time, select Wi-Fi data.

MOBILE HOTSPOT

Turn on your Mobile Hotspot to share your device's data connection with other devices.

1. Go to the Settings on your phone and click Connections and select the Mobile hotspot and tethering option and tap Mobile hotspot.

2. To turn the Mobile Hotspot on select the On button.

3. Turn on Wi-Fi on the other device that you want to share your device connection with, and select your device from the list of available devices then enter the password of the Hotspot to connect to it.

TIP: You can easily connect to a Mobile Hotspot by simply scanning the QR code with your camera.

Configure mobile hotspot settings

To configure the settings for your Mobile Hotspot connection

1. Launch the Settings app on your gadget and click on the 📶 Connections option > press Mobile hotspot and tethering > Mobile hotspot.
2. Select configure.
   - You can alter the default Hotspot name.
   - Choose a security level for your Mobile Hotspot.
   - You can set a password for your Mobile hotspot.
   - Select from the list of available bandwidth options.
   - More advanced Mobile Hotspot settings can be configured.
3. Select the option "Save."

Auto hotspot

With the Auto Hotspot, you can set your device to share your connections to device that are signed into your Samsung account automatically.

1. To work with the Auto Hotspot feature, launch the Settings app and click 📶 Connections > Mobile hotspot and tethering > Mobile hotspot.

2. To turn this feature on, click ⬤.

TETHERING

This feature has similar function with the Mobile Hotspot as it helps to share your device internet connection with others.

1. Launch the app "Settings" and open the Connections tab and click Mobile hotspot and tethering.

2. Choose and alternative:
   - Select Bluetooth Tethering to share the internet connection of your device using Bluetooth.

- Tap USB Tethering to share the internet connection of your gadget using a USB cable from your phone to a computer.
- Touch Ethernet Tethering to share the internet connection of your device with a computer using an Ethernet adapter.

Connect to a printer

Documents and other files can be printed from your phone easily. Just take the following procedures.

1. Open the Settings app and go to the Connections tab and select More connection settings then Printing.

2. Choose a default service for printing and tap More then Add printer.

- Select Download plugin and follow the instructions on the screen to add a print service if your printer needs a plugin.

TIP: This feature is not supported by all apps on your device.

VIRTUAL PRIVATE NETWORKS

With this feature, you can be able to connect to private and hidden networks. Just ask the VPN administrator for the connection info.

1. Launch the app of Settings and go to the Connections page then select More connection settings > press VPN.
2. Select the More options icon and tap VPN profile.
3. Enter the details that you have gotten from the VPN administrator and select Save.

Manage a VPN

From here, you will know how to delete or edit a VPN.

1. Launch the app Settings and go to the menu of Connections then select the More connection settings > tap VPN.
2. Tap the Settings icon close to the VPN.
3. Touch Edit to edit the VPN and touch Delete to remove the VPN.

Connect to a VPN

You will not find any difficulty in reconnecting and disconnecting if you have set up VPN.

1. Go to the device's Settings and select Connections and tap More connection settings > VPN.
2. Choose a VPN and enter the login details and click Connect.
- To disconnect from a VPN connection, tap the VPN and select Disconnect.

SOUNDS AND VIBRATION

Set the sound level of your device to show tap, calls, notifications and more.

Sound mode

The sound mode can also be changed in absence of the volume keys.

- To change the sound mode without the volume keys, find the Settings app, scroll down and tap the 🔊 Sounds and vibration, and then select a mode:
  - Sound: You may alter the vibration, volume levels and sounds that you have selected in sound settings for alerts and notifications.
  - Vibrate while ringing: Your device will vibrate for an incoming call once you turn on this feature.
  - Vibrate: You can allow your device to produce a vibration for calls and alerts.
  - Mute: You can allow your device not to make any sound at all.

- Temporary mute: Set a time limit for your device to remain muted.

NOTE: Use the sound mode to customize the sound levels, rather than using the volume keys.

Vibrations

Set a vibration pattern for your gadget.

1. Launch the app "Settings" and go to Sounds and vibration.
2. Choose from the following options:
- Select a vibration pattern for all calls.
- Choose a vibration pattern for notifications.
- Set a vibration intensity level for calls, taps and notification simply be moving the slider to your desired level.

Volume

To set the volume level for notifications, media, ringtone and system sounds, do the following:

- o While on the Setting application, select the Sounds and vibration icon and tap Volume, the move the sliders to control each sound type.

Use Volume keys for media

You can control your media sound volume with the volume key instead of going to the sound settings.

1. Tap Volume in the 🔊 Sounds and vibration menu in the Settings app.
2. Select Use volume keys for media to turn on this feature.

Media volume limit

When you are using a Bluetooth device, it is advised that you limit the maximum output of the phone.

1. Tap the Volume option under 🔊 Sound and vibration in the Setting application.
2. Tap the Media volume limit under the ⋮ More options.
3. To turn the feature on select the ⬤ On icon.
- To control the maximum output volume, drag the custom slider.
- To require a PIN when access the volume settings, select Set volume limit on PIN.

Ringtone

You can use the default system sound as your ringtone or you can select, from your device system.

1. Find the Settings app, scroll down then tap 🔊 Sound & vibration and tap Ringtone to set a ringtone.

2. Select a ringtone to play a preview of it, or select ➕ Add to add your media file as a ringtone.

Notification sound

For notification alerts, you can make use of the default system sound or choose form your device media files.

1. Go to the Preferences application and click on the 🔊 Vibration and Sound menu then click Notification sound.

2. Touch the sound that you want to use as the notification sound to hear a preview of it.

TIP: You can customize a notification sound for a particular app to know when you have a notification from that app.

System sounds and vibration

You can enable your gadget to make a vibration on screen taps, and charging tone.

- o Open the Preferences app and click on 🔊 Vibration and Sound then select System sound/vibration management.

Sound

- Touch interactions: Enable your device to produce a sound when the screen is touched.
- Screen lock/unlock: Enable your phone to make a sound when it locks or unlocks.
- Charging: Enable your phone to make a sound while a charger is plugged in.
- Dialing keypad: Enable your phone to make a sound when you type words on the keypad.
- Samsung keyboard: Set the device to make sound when you are typing with the Samsung keyboard.

Vibration

- Touch interactions: Enable your phone to vibrate when the navigation buttons are tapped.
- Dialing keypad: Set your phone to vibrate when the keypad is in use.
- Navigation gestures: Set your device to vibrate when you are using gestures.
- Charging: Set your device to vibrate when a charger is connected.
- Samsung keyboard: Allow your device to vibrate when the Samsung keyboard is in use.

NOTIFICATIONS

Configure a notification for apps and other settings on your device.

Notification pop-up style

To change the pop-up style of notification

- o Tap Settings application from the application screen and click Notifications, then choose a pop-up style:
  - Brief: Set your notification color, lighting style and more.
    - Included apps: Configure apps that will show a brief notification.
    - Brief pop-up settings: Set the Edge lighting style and allow notifications to show even when the screen is not on.
  - Detailed: Turn on the default Samsung notification settings.

DO NOT DISTURB

All notifications and call sound are blocked. You can set the Do not disturb to set a schedule for recurring events such as sleep and meetings. You can also indicate exceptions.

- o Go to the app "Settings" and click on the Do not disturb menu in the ![icon] Notification section and do the following:
    - Do not disturb: Turn on the Do not disturb to block sound and notifications.
    - For how long?: When Do not disturb is on manually, you can select a default duration.

Schedule
- Sleeping: Set up a schedule for Do not disturb when you are asleep.
- Add schedule: Make a schedule to edit the day and the time to put your device on Do not disturb mode.

Exceptions
- Allowed during Do not disturb: Turn this on to allow some calls and messages and more.

- Alarms and sounds: While the Do not disturb mode is on, you can activate sound and vibrations for alarms, events and reminders.
- Apps: set apps that you may want to get notifications from while the Do not disturb mode is on.
- Hide notifications: View the customizations options for hiding notifications.

Alert when phone picked up

You will be notified with a vibration from your phone that there are missed calls and messages when you pick it up.

- o From Settings, go to the Advanced features menu and select click Motions and gestures and finally select Alert when phone picked up.

DISPLAY

On the display menu, you can control the brightness of your screen, the font size, timeout delay and many more.

Dark mode

Your eyes are more comfortable at night when your device switches to a darker mode, by darkening the white bright screen and notifications.

- o From Settings, click Display to use the options below:
  - Light: Your gadget comes with a light color theme.
  - Dark: You can make your gadget to be in a darker mode for you to see more comfortable at night.
  - Dark mode settings: Set up when to apply dark mode to your device.
    - Turn on as scheduled: Customize dark mode for either Sunset or Sunrise or Custom schedule.

Screen brightness

The screen brightness can be set to adjust automatically depending on the lighting condition or your own preference.

1. From Settings, go to the 🔅 Display icon menu.
2. The following can be customized when you tap Brightness under Display:

- Drag the brightness slider to either increase or decrease it.
- To control the brightness based on the lighting condition automatically, select Adaptive brightness.

TIP: You can also change the screen brightness from the Quick Settings menu.

Motion smoothness

You will be able to scroll smoothly and have access to more realistic animations because the motion smoothness increases the refresh rate of the screen.

1. Tap Motion smoothness under the 🔅 Display menu in the Settings app.

2. Select an option under the Motion smoothness to apply and click Apply.

Eye comfort shield

You can use your phone more effectively at night when this mode is activated. This feature reduces the eye strain and you can also set a schedule to turn it on or off.

- Find the Settings app, scroll downward and tap Eye comfort shield in the Display menu and choose from the following options:
  - Click the activation button .
  - Tap adaptive, if you want the color temperature of the screen to change automatically based on your pattern of usage and the time of the day.
  - To set a schedule for Eye comfort shield, tap Custom.
    - Choose a schedule and select always on, Sunset to Sunrise or Custom.
    - Move the color temperature slider to set the opacity color filter.

Screen mode

Your device has variety of screen mode options to control the quality of the screen for different conditions.

1. Go to the app "Settings" and click on Display and tap Screen mode.
2. Choose an option to configure a different screen mode you want.

Font size and style

Modify the size and style of your device font to customize your phone.

- o From Settings, click Font size and style under Display.
  - To select a different font, click Font style.
    - Choose from the default fonts or tap to download a font from the Galaxy store.
  - Tap **Bold** for all fonts to appear in bold weight.
  - To alter the size of the text, slide the adjustment button.

Screen zoom

Change the zoom mode for object to be either smaller or larger.

1. From Settings tap Screen zoom under Display.
2. To change the zoom level, drag the zoom slider.

Full screen apps

You are allowed to select which app to use in full screen aspect ratio.

- From Settings, click Full screen apps under Display and tap apps to turn on this feature.

Screen timeout

Create a screen timeout time, so that your phone will go off when it is unused for some time.

- From Settings, select Screen timeout under Display and select a time limit for the screen to go off.

Accidental touch protection

You screen will be prevented from accidental touch when your phone is in a dark place, such as pocket and bag, when this feature is activated.

- From settings tap Accidental touch protection in the ⚙ Display menu to activate it.

Touch sensitivity

Increase the touch sensitivity of the screen to enable it responds to touches properly when you are using screen protectors.

- Launch the Settings app and select the ⚙ Display icon and finally tap Touch sensitivity to turn this feature on.

Show charging information

The battery level will appear on the off screen when this feature is activated.

- From Settings, click on Show charging information in the ⚙ Display screen to show the charging information of your device.

Screen saver

Do the following to show colors or picture when the screen turns off while charging.

1. Go to the Settings application and select Screen saver in the ⚙ Display screen.
2. Choose from the following options, the one to configure:
   - None: Once this is selected, no image or color will appear when the screen goes off.
   - Colors: Tap on the selector to show a changing screen of colors.
   - Photo table: Display all your pictures on the photo table.
   - Photo frame: Display all your pictures in the photo frame.
   - Photos: Pictures can be viewed from your Google Photos account.
3. Click on Preview to see a preview of the screen saver that you have selected.

Lift to wake

Raise your device up to turn on the screen.

- From Settings, tap motion and gestures in the ⚙ Advanced features menu and tap Lift to wake to activate the feature.

Double tap to turn on & off screen

You turn your device screen on and off by double tapping on the screen rather than using the Side button Power button).

- From the Settings application, click on Motion and gesture then tap Double tap to turn on or off the screen in the ⚙ Advanced feature menu.

Keep screen on while viewing

Leave your screen on while it is in use.

- Launch the app for Settings and click ⚙ Advanced features then tap Motions and gestures and finally tap Keep screen on while viewing, and click ⊙ On to activate the feature.

One-handed mode

Change the screen layout to allow you carry out operation on your device with one hand.

1. From the Settings application on your device click One-Handed mode in the ⊙ Advanced features menu.

2. Select ⬤ On to activate the feature.

- Gesture: Swipe upward in the middle part of the down edge of the screen.
- Button: To reduce the size of the display, tap the ▢ Home button twice.

LOCK SCREEN AND SECURITY

Set a lock to keep all your device details secured.

Screen lock types

Choose from the following screen lock types to set as a secure screen lock;

- Swipe
- Password
- Pattern
- PIN

NOTE: You may also use your fingerprint to privatize all your device contents and sensitive data.

Set a secure screen lock

Use on of the screen lock methods that are highlighted above to secure your device. Without them you will not be able to use the Biometric feature.

1. From Settings click on Screen lock under the Lock screen menu and choose a screen lock type that you prefer.

2. To enable all notifications to appear on the lock screen, click ⬤ On. You will see the following options:

- Icon only: Notifications icons with info will show on the lock screen only.

- Details: Notifications will show on the lock screen.

- Transparency: Set the transparency value of notification cards the way you want.

- Auto-reverse text color: Set the notification reverse color text based on the background color.

- Hide content: Don't show notifications on the panel of notification.

- Notifications to show: Choose notifications to appear on the Lock screen.

- Show on Always On Display: Allow notifications to appear on the Always on display screen.

3. To save and leave the menu, select Done

4. Customize the options below for the screen lock:

- Smart Lock: Unlocks your device automatically when a location that is trusted is detected. You need a secure lock screen to use this feature.

- Secure lock settings: You can set your screen lock settings. You also need a secure and strong screen lock for this.

- Always On Display: Configure to turn on the Always On Display screen.

Clock and information

To customize feature and other necessary information that will show on the lock screen, do the following.

- From Setting app, touch 🔒 Lock screen for the following options:

  - Wallpaper services: More features like Dynamic lock screen and guide page can be allowed.

- Clock style: On the Lock screen and the Always on display screen, you can add the color of the clock type.
- Roaming clock: While roaming, you can allow your device to show the time both where you are and at home.
- Widgets: Activate widgets on the lock screen to view necessary information on the lock screen.
- Notifications: Select a notification that will appear on the Lock screen.
- Shortcuts: You an app shortcut to add to your Lock screen.

Google Play Protect

Google Play will constantly check your apps and device for security risks.

- o From Settings app, click Google Paly Protect under ◯ Biometrics and security.
- Your device will search for updates automatically.

FIND MY MOBILE

Activate this feature to prevent your device from loss or theft by locking it and deleting your data remotely. You need a Samsung account to use this feature, and you also need to activate Google location services.

Turn on Find My Mobile

To activate this feature

1. Go to the Settings application and launch the ⭘ Biometrics and security option and tap Find My Mobile.

2. Select ⬤ On to activate the feature and login to your Samsung account.

- Remote unlock: This feature grants permission to Samsung to save your secure screen lock methods so that your device can be controlled and unlocked remotely.

- Send last location: This feature grants permission to your device to share it last location to the Find My Mobile server if the remaining battery depletes beyond a certain level.

Find My Device

Activate this feature to prevent your device from loss or theft by locking it and deleting your data remotely. You need a Google account to use this feature, and you also need to activate Google location services.

1. From Settings, hit the ⬤ Biometrics and security icon and press Find My Device.
   - If you don't login in to a Google account, this feature will not work properly.
2. You will see the following options:
   - Find My Device: If the app is not found on your device by default, you can install it from Google Play Store.
   - Web: You can launch the feature on the Internet browser.

Permission manager

Permit apps to access features like the camera, microphone or location and more.

1. From Settings, click on the ⭕ Biometric and security menu the select tap Permission manager.

2. Click an application to pick which permission you want to be notified about under a category.

TIP: Apps will always ask for permission to certain features of your device when you are accessing them for the first time.

SAMSUNG PASS

Use this feature to view your favorite services with biometric data. Sign in to a Samsung account first to use this feature.

1. Visit Settings, go to the ⬤ Biometrics and security screen and tap Samsung Pass to turn the feature on.
2. Sign in to the account and add your biometric data.

Secure Folder

Add all your files to a secure folder, to protect your device and all the sensitive content from those that may have access to the device. You will have to sign in to a Samsung account first to use the Secure folder.

- From Settings you will have to tap the ⬤ Security and biometric icon and tap Secure folder.

Install unknown apps

With this feature, you can install apps that are an unknown source.

1. From Settings, go straight to the ⬤ Security and biometric menu and select Install unknown.
2. Tap the ⬤ On icon to activate the feature.

TIP: Your phone and its content are opened to risks by allow the device to install unknown app.

Encrypt or decrypt SD card

Encrypt an optional memory card to protect your data. This will allow your info on the memory card to be access with a password.

1. From the Settings application, go to the ⬤ Biometrics and security menu and tap Encrypt SD card to encrypt the SD card.
2. To encrypt all data on the SD card, select Encrypt SD and follow the prompts.

TIP: Once a Factory data reset is carried out on your device, it stops it form accessing an SD card that is encrypted. Decrypt the installed SD card first, before you perform a factory data reset.

Decrypt SD card

Follow the procedure below to decrypt SD card.

1. From the Settings application, go to the ⭕ Biometrics and security menu and tap Decrypt SD card to decrypt the SD card.
2. To decrypt all data on the SD card, select Decrypt SD and follow the prompts.

Set up SIM card lock

Set a SIM card lock to prevent unauthorized use of your SIM card.

- o Visit Settings, scroll down and tap ⭕ Biometrics and security menu and tap Other security settings > tap Set up SIM card lock to turn on the feature.
- Select "Change SIM card PIN" to create a new PIN for the SIM card.

View passwords

To show character of your password as you type, do the following:

- Visit Settings, scroll down and tap ⚙ Biometric & security menu, tap Other settings then select Make password visible.

Printed in Great Britain
by Amazon